Strong Clear & Unapologetic

Midlife Reimagined

10 Principles to Redefine

Strength, Wellness & Leadership

in Mid-Life

by

Sally Thibault

Copyright © Sally Thibault 2025
First print edition published in Canada 2025
eBook edition published in Canada 2025
Author Sally Thibault: Wisemothers Publishing
1500 Howe Street, Vancouver Canada V6Z 2N1
sally@mid-lifereimagined.com

National Library Cataloguing-in-Publication entry:
Thibault, Sally
Strong Clear & Unapologetic: Midlife Reimagined

ISBN 978-0-9807374-6-2

Subjects:
1. Thibault, Sally
2. *Principles to Reimagine - Strength, Wellness & Leadership in Mid-Life*

DISCLAIMER

The author of this book does not dispense medical advice or prescribe the use of any technique as a form of treatment for physical, emotional or medical problems without the advice of a physician, either directly or indirectly. The intent of the author is only to offer information of a general nature to help you in your quest for emotional and spiritual wellbeing. For the privacy of clients - most names, times, dates and some circumstances shared in this book have been changed. All suggestions in the book are educational in nature and for the reader's own self-improvement. While the author is an experienced and certified EFT practitioner and Professional Counsellor, she is not a licensed healthcare provider and does not make any warranty or guarantee regarding the personal use of EFT (Tapping). In the event you use any of the information that you use any of this information in this book for yourself or your clients, the author and publisher assume no responsibility for your actions or outcome.

For my darling granddaughter Ava Patricia

As I writing this book, I am so honoured witness your mother being pregnant with you, I am reminded of the incredible power of a woman's body in growing a little human.

The joy and excitement I feel as your grandmother is extraordinary. From the moment your Mom and Dad told us they were expecting you, on March 17, 2025, to the time I heard your heartbeat, when you were just a little apple size bub at 15 weeks and two days old, to the day all of us fell hopelessly in love with you as you entered the world. Moments frozen in time in my memory, that I will always treasure, and will retell you over and over again... I can because I am your grandmother and that's my prerogative. ☺

My wish for you, is that you never judge yourself, compare yourself or shrink to fit for others; that you always have the confidence to value your self-worth, develop a strong belief in yourself to always chase your dreams and the wisdom to know when to ask for guidance. My hope that you will honour the four generations of the first-born women who came before you, by living your best life in the way you choose.

I will love you for eternity

Gigi

November 2025

Table of Contents

10 PRINCIPLES OF WELLNESS

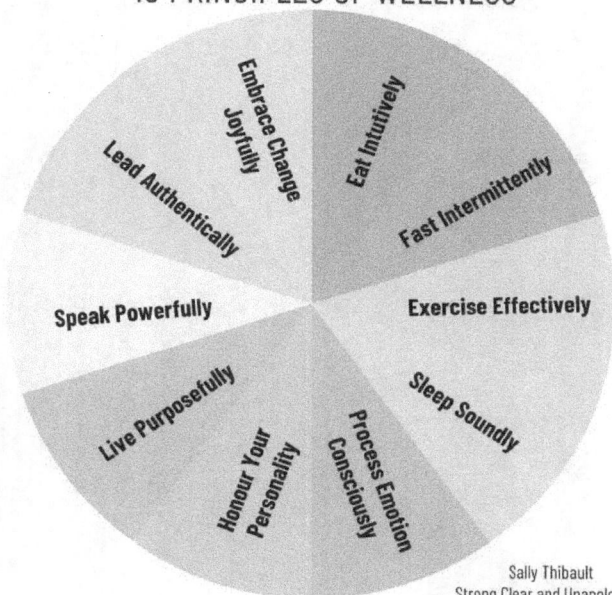

Embrace Change Joyfully

Eat Intuitively

Lead Authentically

Fast Intermittently

Speak Powerfully

Exercise Effectively

Live Purposefully

Sleep Soundly

Honour Your Personality

Process Emotion Consciously

Sally Thibault
Strong Clear and Unapologetic

Introduction

The not so silent revolution

We are living through times of extraordinary uncertainty — socially, economically, politically. And when the ground beneath us shifts, the world instinctively looks for leadership that is steady, wise, and deeply human.

It's no coincidence that in families, in businesses, and in communities — midlife women are quietly and powerfully already holding it all together. And yet when it comes to leadership in politics and business, too many of these same women are stepping back. Or being overlooked. Why?

Because we are not openly talking about the invisible transformation happening to us in midlife — the hormonal shifts that can shake confidence, clarity, and identity.

The problem is we have made strength look like silence. We've made leadership look like pretending nothing is changing, when in fact, everything about us is. Our bodies, our brains and the way we view life and our role in it. A shift of power from strength without – to strength within.

But so many women fear this change, instead cloaking themselves in an invisible armour, protecting themselves from any perceived weakness of their body, their energy and their mind, for fear of being perceived as weak, emotional or not up to the challenges of leadership.

But, what if the very things we've felt we needed to hide, the symptoms, the challenges and the recalibration — are the source of our next-level power?

Because when a woman claims her full self — physically, emotionally, hormonally and all — she becomes a force, not just for herself, but in the boardroom, her family and her community.

Now more than ever, the world needs **strong, clear, and unapologetic midlife** women. Not fearing this stage of their lives but instead embracing this time as the natural progression of time.

You see, midlife isn't the end of our relevance, it is the beginning of a whole new era of confidence, wisdom and intuition.

Let's stop stepping out of the room and start stepping into the power we've earned. Being the change we want to see. Because if we want change, it has to come from us. And owning who we are and who we are becoming is the place to start. It's time to reimagine midlife and change the world at the same time.

Menopause & Midlife

There are three times in a woman's life when she goes through life-changing hormonal changes.

1. **Puberty** – lasts approximately one to three years, and during that time the world seems so strange, your body changes, your breast start to grow (how embarrassing) and you grow hair in weird places (even more embarrassing). Sleep and being with your friends are the most important things in your life. Boys start paying attention to you, for other reasons. Your moods take over your body, and your Mom is so annoying, making a big deal out of your first period – but failing to tell you that it will happen to you about 480 times in your life!

2. **Pregnancy & Postpartum** – lasts approximately 12 to 18 months. 80% of women will experience this change, and even though exhaustion takes over, certain foods make you feel nauseous, and your growing belly expands, there is an immense joy that goes with it. Families celebrate you; strangers are interested in due dates, and you just fall in love with this little human growing within you. After the birth, breastfeeding continues to impact on your hormones, and despite the fluctuating hormones – the 'happy' hormone oxytocin floods your body every time you nurse this little human, making it all so bearable and joyful.

3. **Menopause** – lasts between 10 to 14 years. During which time, your breasts sag, your belly starts to grow, foods that you used to love, now make your belly bloat. You grow hair in weird places, like your chin,

your husband or partner eating suddenly becomes extremely annoying. Sleep becomes disrupted and your body feels like it is betraying you – heating up in the least appropriate moments! Worst of all nobody cares!

And while the first two are treated with compassion, understanding and a great deal of excitement by others, the same cannot be said for the third.

Up until recently there was little to no research, knowledge or discussion about this life changing event that 51% of the population will experience. And with as little as 4% of medical research funding allocated to all women's health, combined with menopause training for doctors almost as an afterthought, rather than studying the up to 40 symptoms that women can experience during their menopause transition, is it any wonder that this life changing time in a woman's life has been largely ignored.

Learning from the Elders - My Mother's Journey

My mother passed away when she was only 57. I was pregnant with my second child at the time, so menopause was the last thing on my mind. But now, after going through my own menopause transition, I can remember small things of what her journey must have been like. I remember her sitting on the deck in the back yard crying for seemingly no reason. I remember her experiencing bad periods, including flooding while she was in the supermarket and feeling so embarrassed because she was wearing white pants at the time. I remember her constantly being on a diet, and nothing working.

My mother was one of nine children, born and raised in New Guinea, prior to World War II. Her mother's family had numerous business interests there, and her mother married a handsome Welshman, the manager of one of the coffee plantations they owned.

She had an idyllic childhood and told us many stories of going to school not wearing shoes, accompanied by the native house help, who she adored.

However, their magical childhood, along with the family fortune, ending abruptly after being evacuated from New Guinea, ahead of the Japanese invasion, to Queensland in 1942. She was granted a scholarship to attend a prominent Catholic boarding school in Brisbane until she finished Year Nine, when her parents asked her to leave school and get a job to help support the family.

My mother was quiet, introverted and hard-working, liked and admired by many of her colleagues and friends. She never said a bad word about anybody, and she detested bad language. Any four-letter word was banned in our house, and I was 10 years old when I learned that the word 'damn', was a word she perceived as a swear word. To this day, whenever I think of that word, it ignites a memory of the taste of my mouth being washed out with Solvol Soap! (A builder's soap used in Australia, with pieces of sand in it to get deep seated dirt out of rough skin!).

She once told me a story about going to our family doctor in her late 40's. He was old-fashioned family doctor, who she highly respected. She asked him to prescribe her anti-depressants, because all her friends were taking them. At the time she was working full time in a stressful job, with the five of us siblings still living at home. My Dad had an all-encompassing job and enjoyed golf and cricket on the weekends. This left Mum balancing both motherhood and career, with little support. Her doctor told her that instead of taking medication, that a better way to deal with her stress was to have a glass of sherry every night after work.

She took at recommendation to heart, and in our house, it became a tradition! My sisters and I often joining Mom for a glass of sherry after work, sitting by the open fireplace in our dining room, talking about our day.

It was one of these nights, and just before her 50th birthday, I asked her what the best thing was about turning 50.

She slowly took a sip of her sherry, gazed into the crackling flames of the open fire and said, *"I'm looking forward to it, I feel so confident now in telling stupid people to just "fuck off".*

My sisters and I nearly choked on our sherry!

I thought it was hilarious then, and my sisters and I talked about it for years later. But now, I get it. I totally understand how menopause impacts on you in so many ways, including your brain. And how you go from caring less about what people think about you, to caring more about what is important to you.

Unfortunately, when I was going through my own menopause journey, the penny hadn't dropped – and I was left on my own to figure it out.

My Journey

Fat, frumpy, tired & cranky - You just need to be more disciplined!

Over the last few years, I have often told clients, *"If I only knew then what I know now – what a difference it would have made."*

Because quite honestly, throughout my menopause transition I often felt I was either dying of some awful disease or heading for early on-set dementia!

I began my fitness career in 1981. I trained instructors, hosted a fitness TV show, hosted an Aerobic class with 2,000 participants, and often taught up to four classes a day. I was all over anything to do with nutrition, exercise and healthy living. Right up until my mid 40's I still ran most days and was very particular about the foods I ate, religiously sticking to low-fat, low-calorie foods and avoiding anything I considered 'fattening!'

But slowly, everything changed. After 15 years in the industry, suddenly I wasn't enjoying teaching as much as I had previously. The industry was changing too, and the requirements for certification increased, meaning more study and attending relevant seminars were needed to stay qualified. At the same time, we were also trying to manage my son's recent autism diagnosis. My role at the gym required me to be opening up at 5:30am to teach the 6am class and often subbing for late afternoon and evening classes, on top of the required study. Those morning and afterschool times became a nightmare, with organising school drop offs, pickups, afterschool activities, homework and therapies. Instead of loving what I did, I found the balance really challenging and I started to resent it. We had to make some decisions about what was best for our family, and me stepping out of my career, for what I thought would only be a couple of years, and being more available for those times when the children needed my attention, seemed like the best choice at the time.

I was fortunate to be offered a totally new career as the Director of Community Relations at the private school my children attended. While I enjoyed the change and the challenge, physically things began to change. I started to gain weight, that I put down to no longer teaching, so I increased my aerobic workouts. I began having trouble sleeping with night sweats that woke me often, and I started forgetting people's names, losing my train of thought in the middle of a conversation, or misplacing my keys or phone on a regular basis, which I thought was happening because I was having to learn so much about this new job. But it was the exhaustion, and mood swings, I found were the hardest – well mostly for my family. One night I came home from work, after an exceptionally long day, the kids were in the living room watching something on TV. There were dirty glasses and bowls and left over wrappers on the coffee table. The dishwasher was full of clean dishes, while dirty dishes were in the sink – and I just lost it.

I locked myself in the laundry, screaming at everybody *"I have had enough!!"* My husband Gerry tentatively said through the door *"What do you want us to do"*, and I yelled back *"I don't know, just do it!"* Everything felt just so overwhelming.

Next day, I took the day off work. I was exhausted and I just felt I was not safe to be around humans – for their safety!

At 2:00pm the Oprah Winfrey show came on, and the topic of the show was on this thing called Perimenopause I had never heard of it. But everything they talked about – mood swings, weight gain, exhaustion, not being able to sleep, brain fog, was explaining in detail what I was going through.

I took as many notes as I could, feeling as if I had found the answers. I wasn't dying of some disease, and I wasn't a candidate for dementia! I was so excited.

Next day I already had an appointment with my gynaecologist; to get the results from blood tests I had the week before, and to try and figure out why my periods were so erratic and heavy. I walked into his office, feeling so confident that I had found the answer. Before he could say anything, I said *"I think I am in perimenopause."*

He looked at me with a condescending look and replied, *"We don't think that's a thing, do we?"* And proceeded to tell me my blood tests showed I was not menopausal, but to ensure there were no internal issues, scheduled me for a D & C to see if fibroids were causing the issues with my heavy periods.

I was devastated. My newfound confidence shot. On a follow up visit, he told me that they did find a mass in my uterus, and while it was concerning, was not cancerous, suggested inserting a Mirena IUD, and to follow up with him in six months.

I sat with his diagnosis for a few days. I just knew there was something else going on. This being the time before the internet and smart phones. I knew I was right, because Oprah told me!

I started reading what I could about women, hormones, and midlife. Dr Christiane Northrup's book – *Women's Bodies' Women's Wisdom,* was one of the most powerful.

I knew I had to look at this differently. The transition I was going through was dominated by hormonal issues and I was not imagining it.

During this time a friend of mine suggested I try acupuncture to relieve some of the symptoms I was experiencing, and it certainly helped. The night sweats became less, and I never experienced a hot flash. I am not sure if it was the acupuncture or the Chinese herbs the acupuncturist prescribed. But I am so grateful for an alternative that helped relieve at least those symptoms.

The night everything changed. - The beginning of the 10 Principles

At the end of 2009, I decided it was time to leave my job. After waking up every morning, excited to go to work, I suddenly I dreaded going every day. I was tired and I just didn't feel like myself. It just never occurred to me, that what I was feeling was hormone driven.

The stress, the expectation, the challenges of working in a school environment where every idea I had for something new, I had to work around the Headmaster and the Board; (to make them think it was their idea!) was hard.

As the Director of Community Relations, my job description was so broad - literally anything that wasn't education related landed on my desk. I had to be across so many aspects of the day-to-day public relations, marketing, past students' association, the Parent's and Friends Association, organizer of major events and creator and editor of all publications! I was also the vice-president of our professional development organization and often presented on school marketing at various professional development days and international conferences.

My job required the ability to multi-task like a boss! Always with numerous balls in the air, I was the 'go to' person when people needed questions answered – in a school of 1200 kids, I now look back on that ability as being something quite unique.

On any given day I would walk into my office at 7:30am with up to five staff members, parents or students standing outside my door ready to ask me questions, with my answering machine blinking with numerous messages. I used to pride myself in being able to answer them all with ease! While I loved working with the children and parents (for the most part) and the whole collegiate atmosphere of a great school, it became exhausting.

Then there was this one day.

I woke up feeling exhausted after yet another night of disrupted sleep. Just getting everybody ready for school and work was challenging. When I arrived at the school and drove into the school carpark, I parked my car and had to focus on just putting one foot in front of the other to walk to my office.

When I got to the administration building, I opened the main door and outside my office there were the usual five or so people waiting to ask me a question.

One by one they started asking questions, and I was struggling to stay focused. When the last parent asked me something very simple, I could not fathom what she was saying. Her mouth was moving, but I couldn't focus on what the words meant.

I started to feel like I had left my body, and I was watching everything happening around me, but I was not part of it.

I just held up my hand and said to the parent "I'm so sorry I am *not feeling well, I need to go home.*"

I honestly don't remember a thing about the drive home, but when I got there, I laid down for a nap and woke five hours later.

Miraculously, I was able to schedule an appointment with my naturopath the next afternoon and after a series of tests, she diagnosed adrenal fatigue. I walked out of her office with $200 worth of supplements, a lecture about coping with stress more effectively, but not a word said about perimenopause.

It was now impacting on every part of my life, including my job. I felt like I had been living with this for years *(and as it turned out I had, little did I know perimenopause could last for 10 -14 years!)* I felt as if I was no longer effective, and I was tired, all the time.

It was time to finish it, I was done. I made an appointment with my boss the next day and handed my resignation in, giving him three months' notice to find a replacement. The saddest thing about it, as I look back on that now, it wasn't the job that I didn't like, it was the lack of understanding of the hormonal challenges I was going through, that made me feel I was not capable – nothing could be further from the truth!

I had been on long service the year before, and during that time, wrote my first book, **David's Gift, Asperger's Life and Love,** the story of our family's journey following our son's diagnosis.

The week I resigned, I hired a PR consultant to help with the launch of the book. What I didn't expect was the incredible interest in the book.

My last day of work was on 31 March 2010, and by mid-April, which happened to be Autism Awareness month, I had appeared on two national TV morning programs, numerous radio interviews and was scheduling requests to speak at workshops, conferences and teacher in-service days.

While all the media attention was wonderful, and a new career was literally unfolding before my eyes, I was still trying to manage, what I then thought was, Adrenal Fatigue. I would wake up in the middle of the night, bathed in sweat, often with heart palpitations, questioning if I was capable of riding this wave. I would rerun the media interviews through my head, wishing I had said this better, or hadn't said that. While it was exciting to have a bestselling book, speaking engagements and the sudden media attention, systems needed setting up and I'd often find myself standing in the middle of our home office, trying to remember how the system I set up the day before worked, and would have to start all over again.

I felt like I was standing on the edge of a huge precipice, toes over the edge, and couldn't figure out how to get from one side of the ravine to the next, without falling into the darkness. Then one night, about six months later, it all changed.

I had been asked to speak at an event called Success and Women Over 50, while feeling both grateful for the opportunity, I was also feeling like a fraud and an imposter.

Why?

Quite simply, while I looked like I was holding it all together, in reality I was an exhausted, overweight, emotional mess. And to make it all worse – nothing in my closet fit me!

I was the heaviest I had ever been. How could I stand in front of all these other women and share my story and look as old and frumpy as I felt?

I tried on every single outfit in my closet. Dress? Out of the question, I couldn't zip it up. Skirt with big blouse? – the weight on my hips made every skirt way to short. Pants? Wouldn't zip up or go over my hips.

With every piece of clothing piled high on the bed behind me, I finally found what I could put together as an outfit.

An old pair of black pants, that I could not button up, but I could weave a piece of elastic through the buttonhole and button to keep them up. A large wide shirt that went over the top of that and a scarf that hid it all!

I looked old, I felt old. And all I could think of was "Is this it? Is this the way it is going to be from now on?"

Driving to that event, I had to do a whole heap of talking to myself to find my centre! Reminding myself that I was there for the audience, not me, and at the same time feeling I like such a fraud. I had been a fitness instructor for much of my adult life, and here I was 20lbs overweight, my skin looking as if I was 10 years older and about to share my story of my early career in fitness and the transition to now. I didn't feel very inspiring at all.

While the night was a success, I sold many books and answered many questions, it wasn't enough to satisfy the imposter living in my brain, and I cried all the way home!

This had to change. Something had to give.

Serendipity in Action

The Right Thing Always Shows Up at the Right Time

While all this was going on, I decided to sign up for a 12-month Business Coaching program, to help me set up systems, and learn about social media marketing. While it was predominately about business, there was a great deal of personal development involved. We were also encouraged to form accountability groups. I was grouped with three other women - Fin from Scotland, Cathy from Western Australia and Susan from New York.

We spoke every Wednesday early in the morning, to accommodate the differing time zones. We became very close friends during this time, all four of us forming great friendship bonds.

Susan was also undertaking a course in the relatively then little-known energy psychology technique called Tapping or known as EFT- Emotional Freedom Techniques.

The more Susan told us about this technique, the less I was interested. It sounded so weird and not at all interesting.

But as she studied more and practised it daily, over the course of our calls, I saw her business and her personal life go from strength to strength.

One day, I was telling the group how I was struggling to get high paid speaking jobs. It seemed I would always get to a certain point of marketing and negotiation, and everything seemed to stop.

Susan asked again, *"Let me do a tapping session with you"*. Reluctantly, and because cash flow was getting very sparse, I said yes.

We set up a skype call the next day and Gerry joined in. After a few rounds of using tapping, I could feel something shift. Like a heaviness was lifted. I recognised that I had a massive limiting belief around worthiness and money. I realised, in the tapping session, that I had been sabotaging myself around money. Not feeling worthy to ask for it and sabotaging myself by not taking up opportunities as they arose. For the speaking engagements I was booking, I would overcompensate, not factoring in the hours of research and presentation preparation required, so that the fee I asked for didn't match the amount of work I did. Sometimes working for as little as $10 or $20 an hour!

During the session we also 'reframed' a new belief about value and worth, that instilled a new confidence around both feeling comfortable about asking for the fees I wanted to charge, and the value I could bring.

Within 48 hours, two things happened, that were too 'coincidental' to just put down to 'coincidence'!

Two days after our session with Susan, I received call from a conference organizer asking me if I was available to take over from a keynote speaker who had fallen ill. First, she asked me if I would speak for free. With my newfound confidence, I said no. I had to honour this new belief I had implemented, with action. And surprisingly, I felt comfortable with my decision. Which was so different to how I would have responded 48 hours before. Somehow this new belief anchored in a whole new way of being. I knew I had to trust, that if I held true to my value and worth, that the opportunities would flow in another way.

The next day, she phoned me again and asked me what my rate was and asked if I could do two presentations for the conference. Without even consciously thinking about it, I quoted her double what I would normally quote, because in saying yes to two presentations meant I only had 72 hours to prepare both, as the conference was the following week. To my surprise she agreed and paid the deposit into my account that night, along with booking plane tickets and hotel accommodation!

The day after that, Gerry, who had been working on a difficult land sale for months, received a call from the seller, offering a cash contract with a 14-day settlement. It was all too coincidental.

I wanted to know more. I researched EFT training, and found a course being conducted the next week, not far from me. And it was in that course that I not only learned the intricacies of the modality – but shifted many long-term beliefs, including a disorder eating belief, I had developed during the fitness industry days.

Those few days of EFT training were incredibly powerful. I watched so many people in that course, change life-long limiting beliefs and release self-sabotaging behaviours. Not only did I shift a few more money blocks but also cleared my disordered way of eating. This proved to be a major step forward for me. All those beliefs from my teenage years about weight and food wrapped up in beliefs about worthiness, genetics and misinformation. It was like trying to unravel an enormous spider web! There were so many aspects, that as I delved deeper, went way beyond food and I didn't realise just how far back those beliefs went or how intertwined they were.

The Menopause Connection

It dawned on me one day, after one of my tapping sessions, that during this menopausal stage in my life, so many limiting beliefs I had been holding since childhood, were resurfacing for me to acknowledge. It felt like I was peeling back layers of an onion. I didn't even realise that many of these beliefs, that were so ingrained in my brain and actions, were limiting what I believed about myself. It wasn't till started to question them, that they began suddenly falling like a house of cards. I remember saying to Gerry one day, after I had done a tapping session - *"Who am I? I don't even recognise me anymore!"* Once I started down the path of self-identifying the limiting patterns in my life, I simply didn't have the emotional bandwidth to carry them any longer.

As I continued to unravel the spider web through EFT, meditation and through journalling, I realised that so much of what we believe about ourselves and our capabilities, is impacted by those words and events of our past. We make up stories in our head about our worth and our value. Ironically, they are the loudest during our menopause journey, where we are at the mercy of changing hormones. Our brain and our body, that we have relied on to support us, no matter what, suddenly feels like it is sabotaging us. And we have a choice, either we deal with them or we don't. I found that, when I identified the negative patterns, and released them, I just felt lighter, more intuitive; the brain fog lifted a little, the anxiety and worry dissipated. That's not to say my menopausal symptoms magically vanished, but what happened was that I could think more clearly, and I felt more in control. I felt more capable of advocating for myself and mapping out strategies that worked.

During our menopausal transition, we are in a powerful transformative time in our lives, evolving into the who we truly are, before life got in the way. It's not a misalignment, it's a realignment! While it may feel like we are losing our edge, what is really happening is that our brain and our body are recalibrating.

I have worked with so many women who believed that this time in their lives signalled the end of their powerful years. Nothing could be further from the truth. This is the time to step into that strong, clear and unapologetic leadership that we inherently know how to do.

Midlife women leaders positively impact on families, communities, government and corporations, and the statistics prove it -

- Companies with 30% women leaders make 15% more profit.

- Women over 45 lead more strategic shifts than any other group

- Midlife women create more inclusive cultures, stronger policies, and better outcomes in business & government.

If there has ever been a time for women to step up into leadership – it is now. There is a massive shift happening on the planet, where the need for midlife women to step into unapologetic leadership is desperately needed. But there must be allowances. Allowances for the hormonal shifts women go through. Because those hormonal changes are not a weakness, but a strength. Not talking about them or trying to pretend they are not happening does not serve women, those who work with them, or those who love them.

Each of our hormonal shifts, brings a power that makes us unique.

Pregnancy, childbirth and breastfeeding, expand our ability to love in ways we didn't think possible. We learn how to multi-task while managing and adapting to pain and sheer exhaustion, all while falling divinely in love with this little human we have created. In the process we become stronger, more compassionate, patient and understanding than we ever thought possible.

Our menopause transition rewires our brain to embrace the wisdom, experience and life lessons that allow us to cut through things that don't feel right.

When women realise how powerful they really are, when the narrative about women in leadership shifts from thinking about hormonal change as a weakness, to honouring them as evolvement, the world can change, families will thrive, business grow and communities ultimately benefit.

In a study published in The Harvard Business Review in November 2025, researchers observed 64 middle-aged peri- and post-menopausal women who held senior leadership positions to see if how they navigated changes associated with menopause. The researchers found that these women used their symptoms as a quest for answers. With many women reporting that overcoming challenges related to their symptoms helped them gain inner strength and new skills.

The study highlighted five aspects

- Advocating for themselves and prioritized self-care + health.
- Building support networks at work and beyond, sharing experiences to build solidarity.
- Letting go of judgment and embracing authenticity.
- Gaining confidence and empathy that strengthened their leadership.
- Using their positions to drive change, from advocacy groups to workplace policies.

Strong, clear and unapologetic leadership, begins with self-leadership. You are not broken, you are entering the most powerful time of your life, and while the seeking advice on the best way to manage the physical symptoms of menopause is important, understanding how you are changing emotionally and spiritually during this time is simply life changing.

So how to do you manage this stage of your life unapologetically? There are four major steps:

1. **Prioritizing your health and wellbeing** as if your life depended upon it. Because it does. Now it's about creating those 'non-negotiable' but flexible boundaries that are the foundations for your energy, clarity and health, not just for now, but for the rest of your life.

2. **Embracing and learning more about the elephant in the room** - the hormonal shifts during our most productive years of our lives. No matter how much you try to ignore or hide this, it's happening. And the more willing you are to acknowledge what you are going

through, the more confident and effective you will become.

3. **Recognising the pain of the people, words and events of your past, and how it has impacted on you.** And that means identifying how that pain causes you to be triggered by situations now that impact on your body, your relationships, and your leadership.

4. **Understanding that strong, clear and unapologetic leadership is feminine.** This is not the stage of your life where you emulate male leadership. This is about living authentically in your power. Women have more power when they lead with intuition and heart, that is our superpower. Because when you lead from your authentic power, speak your truth authentically, and embrace empathy, truly listening and understanding on a deep level, people resonate with you.

Over the next chapters, I will share with you my **10 Principles of Wellness.** The Principles I developed for myself during that time in my life when there were no guidelines. When nobody talked about menopause and the incredible transition we go through. When I was told that gaining weight, feeling exhausted, overwhelmed and just plain old – was 'just what happens to women', and when I was told "we don't think perimenopause is a thing do we?"

Through that deep introspective time in my life, I realised I had to take ownership of this change I was going through and map out a way forward. Nobody else was going to rescue me. As I worked on myself more and cleared the limiting beliefs I had lived with for so long, the path became clearer. I decided what areas in my life I needed to create that change and started to implement the strategies to do it.

Over time these strategies started to morph into clear categories, and I started implementing them in my coaching practice to help others.

Each of the categories deals with different aspects of the 10 Principles.

1. Strong – Eat intuitively; Fast Intermittently; Exercise Purposefully; Sleep Deeply.
2. Clear – Process Emotion Consciously; Honour Your Personality; Live Purposefully.
3. Unapologetic – Speak Powerfully; Forgive Easily; Honour Change Joyfully.

All the Principles are based on science, wisdom and longevity, not quick fix gimmicks, and are designed to embrace the whole of you – a total mind-body approach to your life and your leadership.

The purpose of this book is for you to help you implement strategies and action steps from each of the Principles that resonate with you the most. Perhaps starting with Principles one to four first, giving yourself time and permission to experiment with them and adapt them to suit your needs. While, at the same time, being consciously aware of the next six Principles and how they are impacting on your life and leadership.

Whether you feel it or not – you are a powerful, insightful, wise and talented midlife woman lead er but you simply cannot lead well or live well unless you are well – physically, emotionally and spiritually. The decisions you make today, about your health and wellbeing, will impact on you for the next 50 years of your life. With medical innovations and research continuing to evolve, a woman in her 40's or 50's today will likely live to

100 or longer. But those innovations and research, do not mean you will age well, they mean that they can keep you alive for those years. Many of us have watched the health of our ageing parents decline as they age, reliant on pharmaceuticals and medical interventions. Our parents came from a different time, when they didn't have the knowledge about nutrition, exercise or lifestyle that we now do. What decisions you make today, right now, will determine how you will live those next 50 years after all, it's not the years in your life that matter, it is the life in your years that does.

Your physical, emotional and spiritual health must be a priority – because the world needs your experience, your wisdom and your intuition now, more now than ever before.

STRONG

Principle #1 – Eat Intuitively

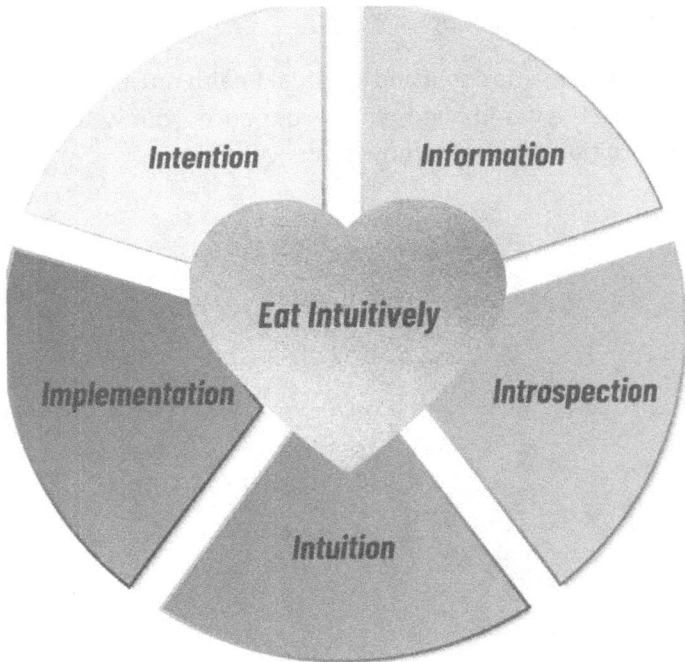

Intuitive Eating was a concept I had embraced for several years, prior to entering perimenopause... you know those days where I could think rationally, and things made sense easily!

I had always been very conscious of my weight, and in my early years of teaching fitness, being skinny was the goal. I watched everything I ate; took skin and fat off chicken and meat. Never touched potatoes or bread and only ate low fat yogurts and cottage cheese, all while teaching four aerobic classes a day.

The universe, I have come to realise, has an enormous sense of humour, in finding my soul mate – a man who honestly believed he could eat anything he wanted and never gain weight.

When we were first together, he would make fun of me and my very restricted way of eating. I would justify it; by telling him he had no idea what it was like to gain weight so easily!

Then one night, he cooked dinner, serving potatoes, vegetables and steak. I watched as he melted butter on his potatoes before pouring sour cream on them. I, on the other hand, had the steak and vegetables and no potatoes, because you know they are fattening! Then he asked me the one question that changed everything. He asked me if I wanted some sour cream on the broccoli, and when I said no, he picked up a teaspoon, put it into the sour cream, held it up and said, *"How could a teaspoon of sour cream put on a pound of weight?"*

I did the normal *"You have no idea what it is like to put on weight?"* response. But the more I thought about it, the more uncomfortable I felt, and the more I realised he made sense.

The next day I watched him make a cup of coffee. He put the kettle on, reached into the pantry, and got two cookies out and put them on a plate. Poured his coffee, walked over to the table and sat down at the chair, having a sip of coffee, followed by a bite of a cookie. Savouring the experience. He was slow and deliberate in his choices.

Then it dawned on me. Because he believed that he could eat anything he wanted, his actions reflected that. He didn't have any emotional charge around those cookies; he just enjoyed them. I realised how different his experience was to mine. I would have eaten two cookies just waiting for the kettle to boil and probably eaten two more when I sat down, then experience the shame and guilt because I ate all that sugar and bad food!

While watching him that day, I wondered what it would feel like if I honestly believed I could eat anything I wanted and not gain weight. What would that feel like? At the time, I was reading Louise Hay's book **You Can Heal Your Life,** where she talked about how powerful our beliefs were and how we can change them to heal any aspect of your life, I wondered if it worked the same way with food and weight.

As I began to question and observe more, I realised a couple of things. I honestly believed that I came from a family with weight issues. I am not sure if anybody actually told me that, but somehow, I just believed that it was a fact. I remember my mother once saying, *"A moment on the lips, a lifetime on the hips!"*, and I believed her. One day, I caught myself saying *'I just have to look at food and I put on weight."* I had probably said it a thousand times before, but now I was taking note of what I was saying, and it really shocked me how often I said things to affirm and lock my belief that food was my enemy!

I slowly began to realise that my self-worth was tied up in the numbers on the bathroom scale and the size of my clothes. The more I uncovered the entangled beliefs about food, exercise, weight and worthiness, the more I realised – I had lost the art of trusting in my intuition to choose foods that were right to fuel my body. I listened to everybody else's opinions about the types of food I should or shouldn't be eating, how many calories I needed to maintain my weight, without ever questioning if it was the right information for me.

If I was to change that – then it had to start with me, in the most basic of ways. To stop allowing those old beliefs to dominate my life and reframe how food was sustenance and energy source not an enemy, while challenging myself to believe at a truly cellular level. I wanted to believe that I was the type of person who could eat anything they wanted, and not gain weight!

Big ask and a bit scary, but other people had cured themselves from all sorts of illnesses through changing their beliefs, then I could too. It was then I decided to take the leap, stop buying into the dogma of diet culture, and trust myself to eat intuitively. To trust in my body, not my emotions, to choose what my body needed at the time, and it worked. For a number of years, I practised Intuitive eating, and my weight and body changed.

But in those tumultuous perimenopause years when I gained so much weight, I had lost my belief in trusting my own wisdom and fell back into the habit of eating emotionally and trying to diet to lose the weight I had gained. Of course it didn't work, but I was in such a muddled way of thinking, I kept trying!

Then the day after speaking at the Women and Success summit, I happened to be looking through some old files in our garage and came across a blog I had written many years before, about the Art of Intuitive Eating, I had forgotten all about it. There it was, in black and white.

I realised, in that totally synchronistic moment, I had really lost my way, and I was ready to try again. But teaching myself to make intuitive decisions about food now, during perimenopause? That was challenging. Gosh I couldn't remember where I left my keys, let alone trust myself to make decisions about food from an intuitive perspective.

Not only are our sex hormones impacted in our menopause transition, but all of them, including – our hunger and satiety hormones – Ghrelin, our hunger hormone and Leptin, our satiety hormone. Both those hormones are less efficient with poor sleep. A weight loss researcher explained to me, that it is almost as if those two hormones swap places when you are not getting good restorative sleep. Making you hungrier and often less sensitive to the natural feelings of fullness!

But trying to diet to lose this weight wasn't working, so I decided that to re-embrace this concept of eating intuitively. But I needed a stronger framework to support me during this transition, creating boundaries that felt safer and more achievable. One day after a workout, it all came to me. Feeling sort of like a download from the universe, I wrote down what I now call - the five aspects of Intuitive Eating.

The Five Aspects of Intuitive Eating

Aspect 1 - Intention – The Power of What and Why

Step one - Make a decision about what you want and why. Most women I coach could tell me everything they didn't want, but when I asked what they did want – I was often met with silence and indecision. Being crystal clear on what you want, helps make sense of the confusion of our menopause transition, when brain fog and stress are high. When you pare down your intentions to just one or two, it helps create clarity.

Ask yourself the question – What do I really want? Answers such as I want to lose weight are not powerful enough to keep you motivated. Instead answers such as "I want to feel strong so that I can..." "I want to have energy so that I can..." "I want to feel confident, so that I can..." are more powerful and create clarity around this change you want to implement.

Step two - Create a vision of what that looks like for you. Imagining a picture of how you want to feel, *(not the bikini picture on the fridge picture)*. What image can you see, when you see yourself with more strength and energy? What can you see yourself doing? How does that energy and strength feel? Create a strong image of yourself in action. Write it down in detail and refer to it every day, until it becomes so much a part of who you are, it feels like you are there already.

Step three - Commit to action. Here I ask my clients to make a promise to themselves to commit to some type of action every day. Small incremental action steps, such as I promise myself to drink two litres of water a day, I promise myself to diarise three workouts a week, I promise myself to look at my vision every day. An intention without action, is just a dream. Amid all the brain fog, hot flashes and sleepless nights, if you can promise yourself to just choose one or two simple intentions to implement the vision you want, you are creating powerful habits, that will build on themselves and last a lifetime.

Step four – Prepare for adaptation. So, here's the deal. Life is going to get in the way. In this process of stepping into a new vision of yourself, there will be days when things do not go according to plan. You are too tired after a disturbed night's sleep; your kids need you to help with an assignment; or you are in the midst of a new project and technology lets you down. That's life. But there are 365 days in a year, 52 weeks in a year, and one challenging day or week is not going to make a difference in the scheme of things. Keep your vision strong, and your action steps simple, being able to adapt to situations is what we mid-life women do best.

Aspect 2 - Information is Power

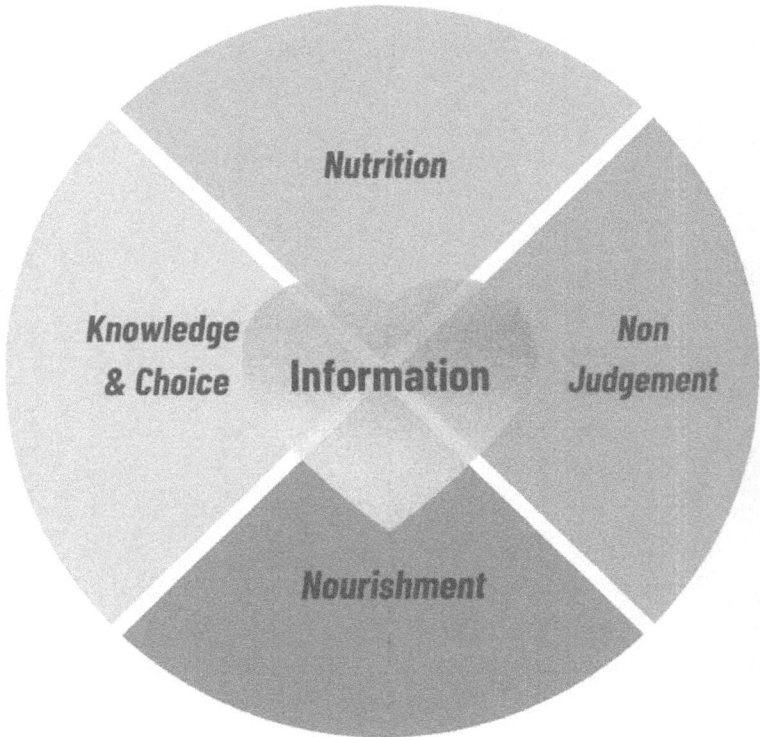

The second aspect of Eating Intuitively is to educate yourself with good information about nutrition. Nutrition that fuels our body, not to keep us skinny, but to help us stay strong and energetic.

When women have the right information, they are a powerful force of nature. We are inherently smart and intuitive and can make our own decisions that are right for us and our family.

But over the years information about nutrition has been hijacked by marketing gimmicks.

Diet culture is no stranger to peddling misinformation. Every decade brings different versions of diet strategies, often paid for by corporations that stand to gain a great deal from perceived 'scientific' studies.

For instance, the concept of 'cereal' for breakfast, was a paid-for marketing campaign by the Kellogg brothers to sell cereal. The low-fat era was based on poorly researched studies that 'fat made you fat'; the processed food industry pushed 'seed oils' as healthier for you, while making processed foods cheaper to manufacture; Large corporate food companies employing food scientists to make ultra-processed foods more flavourful and addictive.

Even today the push to promote fake meat as being healthier for you, while making real meat the villain, has become yet another marketing ploy.

Being informed about the food you choose for you and your family is, I believe the cornerstone to good health and longevity. It requires you to become an avid label reader, going beyond the marketing hype of 'healthy for you', and really knowing what is in the food you buy and eat.

While nutrition can be a whole different chapter in this book, there are a few concepts that can help you make informed decisions, where whole-food nutrition, nourishment of our bodies, knowledge, choice and non-judgement of ourselves, especially during menopause, are the cornerstones thriving through mid-life and beyond. These form the foundation of your *informed* food choices.

Creating simple foundations, takes the guess work out of eating intuitively.

The #1 Menopause nutrient - Protein

I remember working with a client who'd just turned 52. She was doing 'everything right'— eating clean, walking daily, working out with weights three times a week, and implementing intermittent fasting. But she was exhausted, frustrated, and feeling weaker every month.

I asked what she ate on a given day and immediately saw what the problem was. Most days she would start a bowl of cereal and skim milk. For lunch, a salad with perhaps a can of tuna and then for dinner a small piece of chicken or beef (fat or skin removed) She was only eating about 60 grams of protein a day, nowhere near enough for a menopausal woman.

And she's not alone. Most midlife women are unknowingly under-eating protein at the very time their bodies need it most.

Muscle Is Not Just for Looks

Let me be blunt—if you want to age powerfully, protect your independence, and keep doing the things you love, you need muscle.

And muscle needs protein.

After 40, we start to lose muscle mass at a rate of 3–8% per decade. By 50, that loss accelerates unless we intervene. This is why so many women feel like they're "shrinking"—not just in size but in strength, energy, and confidence. It's not age. It's muscle loss.

Muscle is what keeps you steady when you walk, helps you get off the floor, carry your groceries, lift your grandchildren—and quite literally, stand in your power. It's also deeply connected to your metabolism, your immune system, your brain, and even your hormones.

So how do we preserve it? Two ways: resistance training and protein. Consistently. Intentionally. Daily.

The 100g Rule

Here's my simple rule for midlife women: **100 grams of protein every day**.
It's not a magic number. It's a muscle-preserving, energy-boosting, life-enhancing standard that changes everything.

Once you start hitting this number, you'll notice:

- Your energy stabilizes.
- Your cravings decrease.
- Your workouts feel more effective.
- Your body starts reshaping itself in all the right ways.

Think of protein like the bricks for your house. If you're not getting enough, your body has nothing to build with. You're renovating without materials.

But I Don't Want to Be Bulky...

Let's bust this myth right now: women don't 'bulk up' from eating protein or lifting weights. You'd need a full-time training program and specific supplementation for that. What you will get is strength, stability, and a body that feels alive again.

Protein is Your Immune System's Secret Weapon

Protein doesn't just build biceps. It also builds antibodies, enzymes, immune cells. Every time you recover from a cold, heal from a cut, or bounce back after a tough week—it's your protein stores stepping in to help.

In midlife, when immunity begins to decline and stress becomes chronic, protein is like your body's behind-the-scenes warrior. Quietly repairing, restoring, and protecting.

Where to Get Your Protein

I always suggest aiming for at least **30–35 grams per meal**, with a smaller dose as a snack or post-workout support. Here are some of my favorite options:

- **Animal-based**:
  Chicken, turkey, beef, lamb, fish (especially wild salmon or sardines), eggs, Greek yogurt, cottage cheese.

- **Plant-based**:
  Tofu, tempeh, lentils, edamame, quinoa, black beans, chickpeas. (Pro tip: combine sources to get a full amino acid profile.)

- **Supplements**:
  A high-quality plant-based protein powder can fill the gap—especially after workouts or on busy days. My daily protein powerhouse is a smoothie with coconut water, good quality protein powder, a frozen banana, berries, with creatine and collagen for a powerful start to the day.

This Isn't About Perfection—It's About Power

You don't have to track every gram or become obsessive. But you do need to become intentional. Your future self will thank you for every bite of protein you eat today.

Protein isn't just a nutrient. It's our longevity powerhouse to protect against fragility, fatigue, and the lie that we're supposed to decline as we age.

Your Wellness Integration

Reflection:

1. How much protein do you *honestly* think you're currently eating each day?

2. When in your day do you notice the most fatigue, cravings, or mental fog?

3. Have you ever been afraid of eating too much protein or lifting weights? Where do you think that belief came from?

Action Steps:

1. Track your protein intake for seven days—no judgment, just awareness.
2. Aim to include at least 30g of protein at breakfast tomorrow. (Hint: Think eggs, Greek yogurt, protein smoothie.)
3. Choose two protein-rich foods from the list in this chapter and add them to your next grocery shop.
4. Reflect: "If muscle is the key to my freedom, what kind of strength do I want to build—in my body and my life?"

Why Fibre Is the Unsung Hero of Midlife Vitality

I once had a woman say to me, "I'm eating so clean, but I still feel bloated, foggy, and just... stuck."

She wasn't talking about her life (although we got there eventually). She was talking about her gut. Her digestion was sluggish. Her skin looked dull. She felt heavy—even though she was eating "all the right things."

When we looked at her nutrition, there it was: barely 12 grams of fibre a day. Half of what she needed.

The Magic Number: 25–30 Grams a Day (Or more!)

For women in midlife, **25 to 30 grams of fibre per day** is the recommended minimum, especially during hormonal transition.

Why? Because fibre is more than just roughage. It's a metabolic multitasker. It supports gut health, balances blood sugar, feeds your microbiome, and helps with everything from mood to immunity.

Fibre and the Midlife Gut

Let's talk about the gut—and the importance of good gut health during midlife.

As estrogen declines, the gut-brain connection becomes more sensitive. You might feel more bloated, more constipated, or suddenly reactive to foods that never bothered you before. Your microbiome—the trillions of bacteria that live in your gut—start to shift, and without fibre to feed the good ones, the bad guys can take over.

Fibre is like fertilizer for your internal garden. It feeds the beneficial bacteria that produce *short-chain fatty acids*— compounds that reduce inflammation, improve insulin sensitivity, and even support mental clarity.

Fibre and Hormones

Here's what most people don't know: fibre also helps eliminate excess estrogen. When your liver processes hormones, it sends the waste into your gut for excretion. If you're not having regular bowel movements (yes, we're going there), those hormones can get reabsorbed leading to mood swings, breast tenderness, and that puffy, inflamed feeling many women chalk up to "just getting older." This happens because perimenopause involves fluctuating, often high, estrogen levels without the usual balancing effect of sufficient progesterone and can disrupt our body's normal cycles and functions.

Fibre and Fat Loss

Let's not shy away from this truth: many women in midlife are trying to lose that weight that seems to have gone on easily but shifting it again feels almost impossible — but cutting calories and increasing cardio will only making things worse.

Enter fibre.

Fibre slows down digestion, stabilizes blood sugar, and keeps you fuller longer. It reduces cravings and helps your body use fat more efficiently for fuel. In fact, studies show women with higher fibre intake have *less* visceral fat (the dangerous kind around your organs) even if their calorie intake is the same.

It's not about eating less. It's about eating smarter. And fibre is one of the smartest things you can do.

Best Sources of Fibre

There are two types of fibre—*soluble* (which absorbs water and slows digestion) and *insoluble* (which adds bulk and helps waste move through). You need both.

Here are some powerful midlife-friendly sources:

- **Vegetables**: Broccoli, Brussels sprouts, carrots, spinach, kale, beets
- **Fruits**: Berries (especially raspberries), apples (with skin), pears, kiwis, figs
- **Legumes**: Lentils, chickpeas, black beans, edamame
- **Whole Grains**: Oats, quinoa, brown rice, barley
- **Seeds**: Chia seeds, flaxseeds, pumpkin seeds
- **Nuts**: Almonds, walnuts, pistachios

Pro tip: Add a tablespoon of ground flax or chia to your morning smoothie or yogurt. That's an easy fibre and protein boost right there.

One Important Note: Go Slow and Hydrate

If you've been fibre-deficient, don't go from zero to hero overnight. Increasing fibre too quickly can lead to bloating or gas. Add a little more each day—and drink more water. Fibre needs fluid to do its job well.

Your Wellness Integration

Reflection:

1. How regular are your bowel movements? (Yes, these matters—and yes, you need to talk about it!)

2. Do you ever feel bloated, sluggish, or inflamed after eating—even when the food is "healthy"?

3. What's your relationship with letting go? Physically, emotionally, energetically?

Action Steps:
1. Choose one meal tomorrow and add at least one high-fibre food to it.
2. Add 1 tablespoon of ground flax or chia to your smoothie, porridge, or salad dressing this week.
3. Drink 1 extra glass of water for every 5 grams of fibre you add—your gut will thank you.
4. Create your "Fibre Flow List": Write down 5 go-to fibre-rich foods you enjoy and post it on your fridge.

Eat Fat, Stay Sharp

Why Midlife Women Must Rethink Fat—and Stop Trusting Labels

If you're over 45, chances are you grew up during the "low-fat" craze. We were told to ditch butter for margarine, avoid egg yolks, and fear fat like it was poison. Somewhere along the line, we internalized the message: *fat makes you fat.*

It wasn't just wrong. It was harmful.

Because here's the truth: **your hormones, your brain, and your joints are literally made from fat.** And the right kinds of fat are essential to thrive through midlife.

But the wrong kinds? Especially the sneaky, industrially processed ones that hide in "healthy" labels? Those are silently stoking inflammation, increasing brain fog, and hijacking our metabolism—and most women don't even know they're eating them every single day.

Let's clear this up once and for all.

The Good Fats: Your Midlife Brain & Hormone Fuel

Good fats are foundational to vibrant health in midlife. They help:

- Stabilize mood and reduce anxiety
- Support cognitive clarity (a big one for brain fog!)
- Build healthy hormones
- Absorb fat-soluble vitamins (A, D, E, and K)
- Reduce systemic inflammation

The best ones to focus on:

- **Avocados & avocado oil** – rich in monounsaturated fats and vitamin E
- **Olives & olive oil** – the Mediterranean miracle, packed with antioxidants
- **Fatty fish** – salmon, sardines, mackerel; high in anti-inflammatory omega-3s
- **Eggs (with the yolk!)** – a perfect hormone-supporting food
- **Grass-fed butter or ghee** – a nourishing fat full of fat-soluble nutrients

- **Nuts and seeds** – in moderation, these offer good fats plus fibre and minerals
- **Coconut oil** – a stable saturated fat that can be helpful for cooking

These fats don't just keep you full. They help you think more clearly, move more freely, and age more powerfully.

But Then Came Seed Oils…

Here's where things went off track. After World War II, there was a surplus of crops like corn, soy, and cotton. Big food manufacturers saw an opportunity: take the cheap byproducts of these crops, extract the oils, and sell them as "modern" alternatives to animal fats.

Using high-heat chemical processes—including bleach and deodorizers—they turned these unstable oils into what we now know as:

- Canola oil
- Soybean oil
- Corn oil
- Sunflower oil
- Cottonseed oil
- Safflower oil
- Grapeseed oil

They marketed them as *heart-healthy*, but they were never designed for human consumption. These oils oxidize easily, creating harmful compounds in your body. They're high in omega-6 fatty acids—something we need in small amounts—but when consumed in excess (like we do today), they fuel chronic inflammation.

And chronic inflammation in midlife? That's a recipe for:

- Increased hot flashes
- Weight gain (especially around the middle)
- Joint pain
- Brain fog
- Autoimmune flare-ups
- Mood instability

Here's the Problem: They're *Everywhere*

Seed oils are cheap. So, they're used in almost all packaged foods—even ones labeled as "natural," "gluten-free," or "low carb." You'll find them in:

- Salad dressings
- Granola and protein bars
- Breads and crackers
- Restaurant meals
- Frozen meals
- Nut butters
- Vegan snacks
- Non-dairy milks

Even those "health halo" snacks often sneak in sunflower or safflower oil. If it's in a packet, flip it over and read the label. Your body deserves better.

The Midlife Shift: Inflammation is a Dealbreaker

Midlife is an inflammatory tipping point. As estrogen drops, our ability to buffer inflammation also drops. What you *could* get away with in your 30's now causes many menopause symptoms to escalate. Aching joints, mood swings and the weight gain that just won't shift.

Seed oils are like gasoline on that fire.

When you replace them with high-quality fats, you're not just changing your food. You're changing your cells. Your hormones. Your ability to feel grounded in your body again.

✧ Your Wellness Integration:

Reflection:

1. Were you taught to fear fat growing up? How has that shaped your food choices over time?

2. Do you notice a difference in how your body feels after eating healthy fats versus packaged snacks or fried foods?

3. Where might seed oils be hiding in your pantry or regular meals?

Action Steps:
1. Do a pantry check: highlight any oils or products containing canola, soybean, corn, cottonseed, sunflower, or safflower oil.
2. Replace cooking oil with a clean fat like olive oil, avocado oil, or coconut oil.
3. Choose one day this week to focus on eating anti-inflammatory fats at every meal. Write down how you feel at the end of the day.

Aspect 3 - Intuition – The Art of Trust

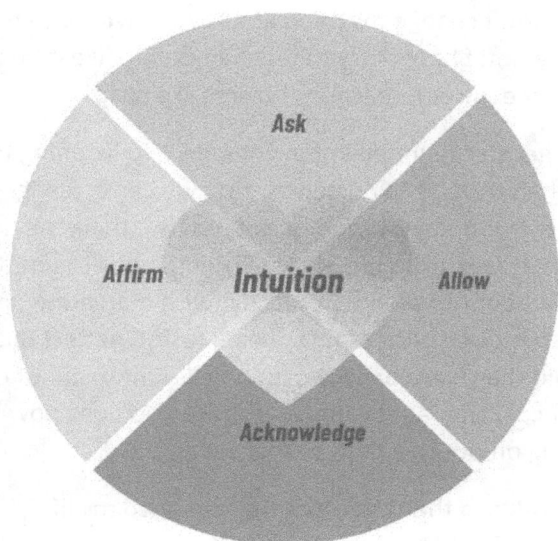

Now you have the knowledge; the next step is to implement what you have learned wisely. To practise the habit of taking that information and learning how to trust in your own intuition in making the right choices for you. Here are the four steps to help you create powerful guidelines to embracing this life changing and energy enhancing concept of Intuitive Eating!

Step One – Allow – Trust in Yourself

The first step is to let go of all the rules you have been following all your life and *allow* your body to make the decision. Most diets are based on a cookie cutter, one size fits all model, as if each of us is the same.

We are not. Honouring your individuality is your superpower, and what works for your best friend may not work for you. My husband and kids love the herb Coriander for instance, I can't stand it, and neither can my brother and sisters. I don't care how many times somebody tells me how good coriander is for you – it won't change my mind at all! Am I wrong to not like it? Of course not. Should I try to teach myself to like it because it's good for me? Absolutely not, it tastes like soap!

We can get so caught up in food trends, and listening to others, rather than trusting in ourselves, that we can often ignore the messages our body is trying to send to us. I think the 'low fat' era was a classic example of that. Taking foods like butter or olive oil out of our diet, to replace it with margarine or seed oils, even though butter and olive oil tasted better! But we were told they were bad for us, so we learnt to adapt our preferences. The ramifications of those decisions now impacting on our health in so many ways.

So, I introduced the statement that changed my life! *"I now allow myself to eat anything I want!"*

After decades of following rules that other people made up, one of the biggest challenges I faced was giving myself permission to eat what I wanted to eat, without the good/bad rules I imposed on myself, when making food choices.

How many times have you stood in a coffee shop, and perused all the cakes, muffins, croissants or pies that you look over to order your coffee, and before you make a decision what to buy, you are calculating which has less calories, fat grams, sugar, good/bad food, or whatever? This journey is letting go of all of that and simply allowing yourself to make the choice because you would really like to eat whatever you choose, without judgement.

Have you ever noticed that when you think you cannot have something – the more you want it? So here it is in reverse.

What would happen if you allowed yourself to eat what your body really needed – instead of fighting the desire all the time?

Step Two - Ask - Your Body Not Your Brain!

So, time to ask the question *"What does my body really need right now?"* This is where you are going to step right out of that head of yours and into the feeling in your body.

I know this is the hardest part. Listening to what your body is telling you and trusting it, rather than making decisions from what you *think* you should be eating or filling up an emotional need.

Women who have lived in restricted eating for years find this tough. We have learned to deny ourselves, because somebody told us that something was good for us – and we believed them – whether it was right for us or not. But remember you are a divine individual and your body is unique. What somebody else says is right for them, may not be right for you. This step is re-learning how to trust in your own body.

I acknowledge this can be a difficult thing to do throughout our menopause transition, especially when Grehlin, Leptin and our stress hormone, Cortisol can be wreaking havoc, but when used in conjunction with the other three steps AND you commit to doing the inner work especially during this time, trust in yourself and the results will surprise you.

Step Three - Affirm – Believing in Yourself!

Intuitive eating is all about choice. The choices you choose to make about the food you choose to eat.

It's deciding how you are best going to support your body, without judgement. Not because somebody tells you what to eat, but because you are choosing the outcome you want.

The greatest gift you can give yourself, is to affirm your choice and honour your body, without judgement. *"I choose to honour the messages my body sends, without judgement".*

Our body sends us messages all the time, and when we judge those messages, we judge ourselves.

Just because you want to eat a piece of chocolate at 10am in the morning does not make you a 'bad' person. Although there would be some people/programs that judge you for that.

You are not a good or bad person because of the food you choose to eat, but the choices you make tell a story. Our choices about everything in life, food or not, are always about how we value ourselves – from what we put up with in our relationships, to whether we choose to exercise or not... and everything in between.

What you choose to eat, will tell you more about how you value yourself than anything else.

As you learn more about you, by doing the inner work we will talk about in the following chapters, the decisions about the food you eat will evolve.

Rather than judging yourself and the messages your body is sending you, question the origin. Is the food you are choosing based on an emotional need not met? Are you choosing certain foods because you cannot speak your truth or feel frustrated about your life? Are you exhausted and tired and just want something sweet to feel better? Do you feel you are not being heard?

Most women who have dieted, have chosen to turn off that mechanism and make it all about calories or fat grams, or macros, depending on what decade you are talking about.

This step is about learning to honour this one body you have and how you choose to honour it. But that cannot happen separately. It goes hand in hand.

The choices you make in this section become the focus of your intention. And yes, you can practise intuitive eating as well as intentional eating. Because once you make the decision to change your life, without feeling like you must live in restriction or you are following rules, then your mind and your body begin to work together. Intentional and Intuitive eating is never about restriction – is it always about your choice. What you want, based on how you value yourself.

Step 4 Acknowledge – How to Listen to Your Body

A huge part of listening to your body, is getting to know and acknowledge how certain foods impact on your body.

This is especially true through our menopausal transition. With changes in estrogen and subsequent changes to our gut microbiome, it may suddenly feel that foods you used to be able to eat and tolerate, have become just the opposite.

Self-leadership is listening to those messages and acknowledging them, not ignoring them!

Bloating, excess gas, joint pain, inflammation, weight gain are the ways your body is trying to tell you something. Are the foods you are eating impacting on your body? Your job is not to ignore it, but to get curious. Just because you used to be able to eat gluten, dairy or sugar ten years ago with no problems, doesn't mean they are not impacting on you now.

For me there are three foods that send me powerful messages, that for years I ignored.

1.Wheat - as much as I love bread and pasta, it makes me feel bloated and gives me pains in my stomach.

I discovered an intolerance to wheat, or gluten or pesticides (who knows which one it is) after my daughter was diagnosed with leaky gut. When the naturopath suggested she stop eating was anything with wheat or gluten. She was devastated – the staple food in our house was bread and pasta! So, to support her, I said I would follow it too.

Within a few days of cutting out wheat and gluten, I couldn't get over how much better I felt. I did not experience bloating or pains in my stomach, that I just thought were normal after eating meals. The other thing I noticed was that I felt more focused and had less brain fogginess – bonus!

2.Dairy – This was a tough one to acknowledge. I loved cheese. Especially a piece (or 10) of beautiful double cream Brie cheese with a glass of champagne, or lashings of parmesan on top of pasta. But one day, I was going through all the videos I had filmed over the years and noticed that in some videos my face looked puffy and I looked older. I could not figure out why, until one week, I was filming videos over two days for an on-line program. The videos I filmed on day one looked fine... but the videos I filmed on day two were totally different. I looked like I hadn't slept all night! It was then; I made the connection. After filming the first videos, Gerry and I had a glass of wine with cheese and crackers! *Nooooo!* I very unwillingly made the connection! Cheese caused inflammation in my body *(it didn't help when I was drinking wine either!!)* that caused my face to look puffy and old! I also realised that the day after eating dairy, I often felt sluggish and my workouts were harder. Damn!

3.Sugar – This was an easy one. It didn't take me long to realise that if I had too much sugar, I would feel jittery and anxious (cranky - the kids would probably call it!) One of my favourite things to do, when the girls were teenagers, was to take them shopping and then have lunch. Lunch usually consisted of a smoothie from a popular, national juice bar, with two pieces of salmon and avocado sushi rolls. But every time I would have these combinations – within 10 minutes of finishing it, I would start to shake. At first, I thought it was because they put too much ice in the smoothie, so I asked for the smoothie without ice. It made no difference.

Then one day, a friend of mine told me about The Calorie King website, that listed all the sugar contents of every food – including takeaway foods. So, I checked out what I was eating, on the site.

OMG – the smoothie I was ordering had 68 grams of sugar per serving AND each sushi roll contained 6.3g of sugar. The average amount of sugar recommended by the WHO is 26 grams of added sugar per person, per day. So, while I thought I was ordering a healthy lunch I was consuming 80 grams of sugar - almost four times the recommended daily amount!

Even though, I am not crazy about eliminating all sugar – that would be incredibly boring – I do make informed decisions and choices about sugar.

That is what being Strong Clear and Unapologetic is all about. It is about making the connection, based on acknowledging the messages your body is sending you – without judgement.

For years I lived with discomfort, because whole wheat bread was good for energy, and dairy was a good source of calcium. I also ignored the messages of hunger or told myself that I needed to eat the 'super foods', the low-fat foods, or the low carb foods, depending on what decade it was, because that's what I was told was the right thing to do.

The true art of this journey is to reteach ourselves how to feel, not only how food impacts on us, but whether we are using food to numb an emotion.

And right there is the problem – if you have used food to not feel an emotion, then you can't feel how food physically impacts on you, because you are disconnected from both the food and the feeling.

That is why this is a journey. It takes time, time to be truly connected to your body, mind, heart, and soul. To stop treating your body as if it some foreign entity that has a mind of its own. It does not - it is part of you.

While I have shared how certain foods impact on me – they may not be the foods that impact on you. If you are struggling with certain symptoms, please seek out a nutritionist or naturopath, to do a food sensitivity or allergy test. Knowledge is power!

However, even though I know these foods impact on me the way they do – that does not mean I don't have them some of the time. I am not going to get into restriction or be obsessive about food choices. But I will allow myself to eat anything I want, I ask my body what it feels like, I affirm that I am making a choice and acknowledge that I will live with the consequences - see it works both ways!

Listening to your body with respect, choosing foods that honour your value, shifting away from denial and relearning how to truly enjoy food just for its taste, can be challenging. But isn't that so much easier than living in restriction for the rest of your life?

So, here's how it works….

1. **Allow** - "I now *allow* myself to eat anything I *want*"

2. **Ask** - "What does my body really *need*?"

3. **Affirm** - "I choose to honour my body *without judgement*"

4. **Acknowledge**– How does this food make my body feel?

Once you master the formula - it works in other areas of your life.

Money

1. **Allow** – "I now allow abundance of money to flow in my life"

2. **Ask -** "What activity will I commit to right now to make this happen"

3. **Affirm -** "I choose to honour my value and worth without judgement"

4. **Acknowledge** – Am I practising an abundance mentality?

Career

1. **Allow -** "I now allow myself to have a career that involves everything I love to do"

2. **Ask -** "What action do I need to take to make this a reality?"

3. **Affirm -** "I choose to believe that my perfect career will happen at the perfect time without judgement"

4. **Acknowledge** – How does it feel to visualize myself in my perfect Career?

Relationships

1. **Allow** "- I now allow the 'perfect for me' partner in my life.

2. **Ask** – "What do I need to do to meet them?"

3. **Affirm** – "I choose to trust that it will happen in the right time, and in the right way, without judgement."

4. **Acknowledge** –Who do I need to become to attract my perfect partner in my life?

See Page 223 for instructions on how to use an EFT/Tapping Script to help implement Intuitive Eating more effectively.

Aspect 4 - Introspection – Understanding You

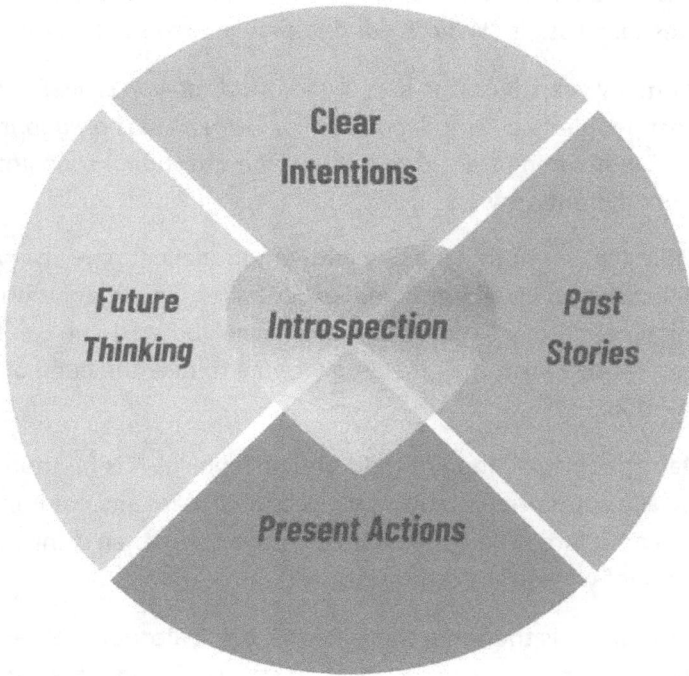

When Food Becomes More Than Sustenance.

Our menopausal transition is so much more than the physical symptoms of hot flashes and brain fog. And while it can be a spiritual and emotional rollercoaster, it is the time for releasing past stories that impact on our current actions, especially around food. This next step in being confident in eating intuitively, is understanding how, in the past, we have used food when we couldn't speak our truth or created comfort for us when we felt scared or unseen. How food became solace or a refuge for us, and how the stories from our parents or grandparents, impacts on both our food choices and our body.

When clients first start working with me, one of the first questions I ask is *"What is your go to when stressed food?"*

For many years I used to ask, *"What foods do you crave?"* and most people said *"Nothing really"* or *"When I was pregnant I......"* but when I started to reframe the question, I soon got a very different answer.

While there is nothing wrong with emotional eating – after all eating should be an emotional experience – joy, celebration, enjoyment etc. It's those foods that once you start you can't stop eating foods, that are simply trying to take the edge off an emotion.

Many people use food as their 'drug of choice'. It is far more socially appropriate to buy a block of chocolate and eat it in the car before picking the kids up from school, than drinking a bottle of wine in the school carpark!

But really, it is the same thing. People drink alcohol in excess to numb an emotion. Our *'go to when stressed'* food is the same.

The Intuitive Eating journey is all about separating what food really represents for us. So, you start to re-learn how to make food choices to satisfy a physiological need from an emotional one.

Each choice holds a brilliant clue to understanding your relationship to food. It contains such gold, that really discovering the cause of the desire, is so empowering.

Using food to solve an emotional need never works, in fact it makes you feel worse. Because while you will feel good for a moment, once that packet of whatever is empty, you will still have to deal with the emotion!

In my first EFT training, we did a session on food cravings. There have been numerous studies done on the subject and learning how to help people get to the emotional cause of food cravings and overcome it was a topic I found fascinating!

I had never thought of a food craving as having an emotional connection to something that happened in your past.

For the exercise, we were paired with another participant. The first question was *"What food do you crave?"* – I couldn't for the life of me think what. Until it was reframed for me – '*What is the food you don't buy, because once you start eating it you can't stop"*

The first thing that came to my mind was Cheese Twisties (like Cheezies in North America!). I wouldn't buy them, because when I did, once that packet was open, there is no going back.

My tapping partner then asked, *"Can you remember a time, where you felt that there wasn't enough food for you?"* Hmmm, I had to think for a minute, but then a memory popped up from my fourth birthday party. *(Honestly, I wonder how so many old memories are still stuck in my brain, when I can't remember where I left my phone five minutes ago!)*

My mother never bought junk food when we were kids. Ice cream was reserved for birthdays, and things like chips were only bought on very special occasions, such as parties or Christmas.

At my birthday party, I clearly remembered Mum putting a large packet of Cheese Twisties into a bowl and then telling me to share them with everybody at the party. By the time I had shared that bowl with all the guests... there were none left for me. I remembered being so heartbroken!

That early memory taught me that if you didn't hurry up and eat those Twisties, they would be gone. No wonder once I opened the pack I couldn't stop eating it, I was scared I there wouldn't be any left for me!

My tapping partner, then asked me to identify the emotions I felt when I recalled the story, where I felt it in my body I felt them, then to measure each emotion on a scale of 1–10. We tapped on many – from sadness, to anger, to disappointment. At the start, most of the emotions had a rating of a 10, and we tapped until each emotion came down to a two or less.

When she was satisfied that each of the emotions no longer rated above a level two, she asked me to reach into the bag and take out a Twistie, smell it, then take a bite. Suddenly, those Twisties, which at the beginning of the tapping session, tasted and smelled so inviting – smelled like chemicals and tasted even worse!

I couldn't believe it when I threw them into the garbage bin, they made me feel sick to my stomach!

Once you remove the emotional connection to that memory, you then only taste the real ingredients. In this case of the Twisties – the only thing I could taste was chemicals, nothing in them was actually real!

I have seen this happen so often now. How the use of EFT to release the emotional food cravings is so powerful. Suddenly chocolate is too sweet, Chips too salty and cheese too fatty! It's extraordinary.

More about EFT in Principle #5

In my experience I have found that there are four main categories of food that people reach for to satisfy an emotional need. And each of those food types has an emotional meaning that once understood reduces the desire dramatically.

Quite simply, you gain control, rather than the food having control over you!

Chips, crackers, crunchy chocolate that contain less chocolate and more crunchy fillings, such as honeycomb, wafers or nuts.

If your *'go to when stressed food'* is always crunchy type food, this may indicate that you are holding back from speaking the truth.

You may not want to, or feel safe to, speak your truth. Perhaps you are feeling angry or frustrated, annoyed at life. Perhaps you are trying to keep the peace in a relationship. Perhaps you feel you are never heard. Perhaps you find it hard to communicate with your boss, or a frustrating team member.

Think of crunchy foods as masking not being able to use your voice as you would like.

Bread or Cakes

Simple carbohydrate food – such as bread or cakes create serotonin, our 'feel-good' hormone.

The desire for simple carbohydrates is often that need for a quick pick up, when you are tired and life feels too hard. This can certainly be the case throughout perimenopause when sleep disturbances often cause you to crave quick energy, and easy to digest foods such as donuts, muffins, croissants etc. To combat this, if you have had a disturbed night's sleep make sure the first meal of your day is high in protein, and carry easy to eat foods high in protein, such as protein balls or cheese if you can tolerate dairy. But also ask yourself, do I have too many choices to make? Does everything feel just darn hard right now? Do I feel unsupported, and overwhelmed?

Smooth, Creamy, Sweet Foods?

Is your *'go to when stressed food'* always sweet, creamy foods that do not require a lot of effort to eat?

Foods such as smooth caramel chocolate or ice-cream can be the go-to food when you do not feel loved or appreciated. Do you have way too much going on in your life and it is all up to you? Do you feel that you must do everything in your own? Are you in a relationship where you do not receive acknowledgement from your partner? Do you feel that you are the one in the family who supports everybody else?

A desire for sweet creamy foods, is often experienced by people at the end of their day. For many mothers, it is the time when you finally get the kids into bed after all the after-school activities, supervising homework, preparing dinner, cleaning the kitchen and finally getting them all to bed.

It's that *"I'm done"* type of emotional eating, that causes so many sleep issues by the way – as eating high sugar foods impacts on blood sugar levels. Causing a blood sugar spike followed by the subsequent blood sugar drop five or six hours later.

When our blood sugar levels drop, the hormone cortisol is called into action to regulate it. Cortisol is also the hormone we require to wake us up in the morning! It is also our stress hormone! Ever wake up at 2am in the morning worrying about something? Check if you have eaten something sweet before you went to bed... you may find the answer!

Cheese

If your *'go to when stressed food'* is cheese, you often indulge in cheese when we have a need to release stress, particularly after a long or challenging day. Cheese contains an amino acid called tyrosine that, when broken down in our bodies, makes us feel content. The fats in cheese also encourage our brains to produce dopamine, a natural feel-good chemical released in our brains' "reward centres".

So, if you are the type of person who loves to eat cheese and crackers before dinner or find yourself eating so much cheese before dinner – that dinner doesn't happen – ask some questions. Am I feeling happy and content in my life right now? Am I doing what I love? How confident to do I feel in my leadership? Am I following my purpose?

Uncovering your food triggers is a powerful aspect of your menopause journey and relearning how to confidently trust in your own body. It's the time in your life to heal that relationship between food, weight and your body, because it is so tied to the intuitive, wise being you are embracing. This is the process of releasing the weight that no longer serves you, first emotionally and then physically.

This is such a powerful aspect of your menopause transition. Right now, you are going to gain weight, feel tired and anxious and have trouble sleeping. That's part of the story. But it's also not accepting the status quo. It's about minimising the impact of menopause symptoms have on your daily life and leadership. Your gut microbiome and brain are changing to adapt to the changes in your hormones. It's about creating a new future story, so that you are not tied to that past story and can rewrite a new one. Recognising that the foods you have *always* eaten in the past that don't serve you anymore, are trying to tell you the truth. They are trying to give you the solution. This is the time to tune in and recognise where the dogma and food rules have impacted on you. Where your own beliefs about your body came from. Menopause is that waking up time. Your body awareness and your body acceptance during this time, will go a long way to embracing this change, instead of fearing it.

How good is that?

Aspect 5 - Implementation – Making It Easy

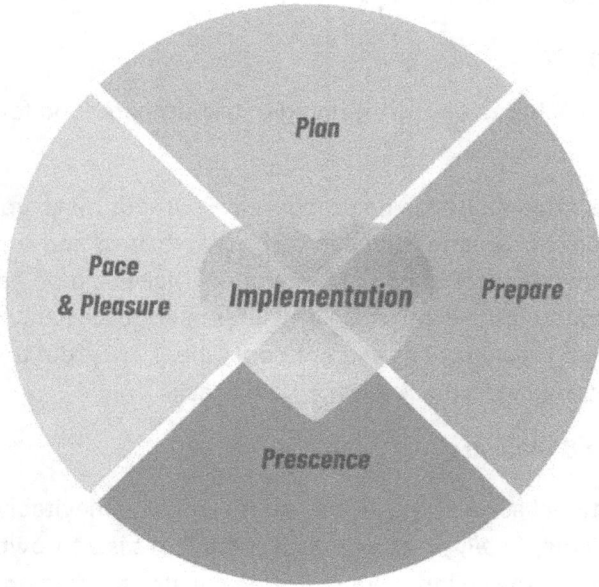

Plan

Pace
& Pleasure · Implementation · Prepare

Prescence

The final step in the Eating Intuitively principle is about the implementation of a new way of eating.

Mid-life women are busy people. Often juggling so many balls in the air – raising teenagers, caring for elderly parents, focusing on job and career, and it can be exhausting. So, creating a system for eating well, requires some thought. Below are the five aspects of Implementation.

1. Plan

Each week, decide what your menu will be for the week. Get the family involved in this. I know many of my clients who have a roster where each family member takes a turn in cooking a meal each week. And in that process, make sure that you are also purchasing enough that can be used for leftovers for lunches or snacks.

2. Prepare

Plan a few hours on the weekend to pre-prepare food for the week.

Decide what meals can be precooked – perhaps make up a Spaghetti Bolognaise, that can be frozen, thawed and cooked, and only the pasta to boil before eating. Make Salmon Patties, that you can put in the fridge and later heat quickly. Buy a large packet of chicken wings and pre-cook, these are great to have in the fridge for a quick high protein snack.

3. Pace & Pleasure

Every time I ask a client, *"How fast do you eat"* inevitably they will tell me, *'really fast'!* Honestly, I think this is a throwback from us raising children, where often we ate standing up, or ate quickly just so our food would not get cold!

Slowing down your pace of eating, allowing up to 20 minutes helps your 'satiety' hormone, Leptin kick into place and register those feelings of fullness, so you are not tempted to overeat.

In many European cultures, food represents a time to come together as a family or a community, and to revel in its wonderful tastes and textures.

A friend of mine moved to Spain in 2024 and one of the highlights for her, was the way in which the Spanish people come together to enjoy long lunches or dinners, shared over a glass of wine. Much of the food is locally sourced and there are very few processed foods...and very few overweight people.

4. Presence

All too often, we are disconnected from food. Eating breakfast on the run or in the car, lunch at your desk or dinner while watching TV. Our body requires a large amount of energy to digest food. And our fast-paced way of disconnected eating, often leads to digestive issues such as heartburn. Be present with food when you eat it. Resist the urge to grab fast food and eat without being mindful. Your body and your health will thank you for it!

STRONG

Principle #2 Fast Intermittently

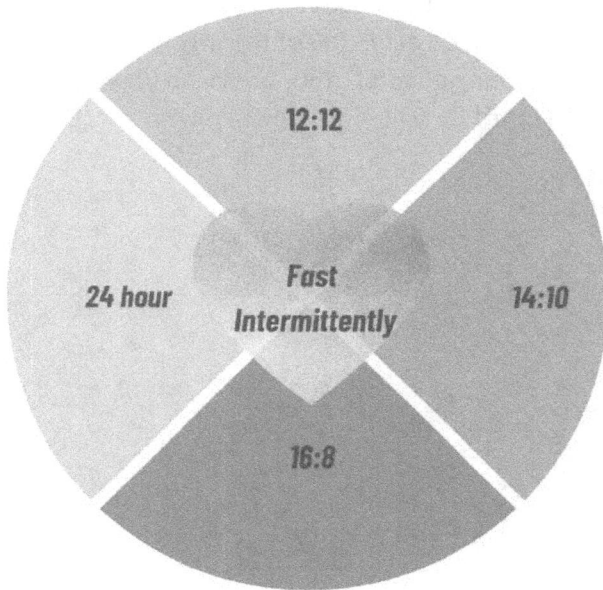

For many women, the word "fasting" conjures up images of deprivation, diet culture, or punishment. But intermittent fasting, when practiced with awareness and flexibility, is *not* about starvation. It's about restoring harmony with your body's natural rhythm—especially during midlife, when that rhythm is changing.

Let's unpack why intermittent fasting can be a game-changer for women in their 40s, 50s, and beyond.

Why Midlife Women Benefit from Intermittent Fasting

In our reproductive years, our bodies are finely tuned to store fat for potential pregnancy. As estrogen begins to decline in perimenopause and menopause, the metabolic advantage we once had begins to shift.

You may experience menopause symptoms more intensely

- More stubborn belly fat
- A drop in energy
- Slower recovery from workouts
- Increased inflammation
- Disrupted sleep

Intermittent fasting supports our physiology during this time by:

Balancing Blood Sugar and Insulin

Fasting periods give the body a break from constant digestion and insulin resistance. Insulin resistance is a condition where cells in your body become less responsive to insulin, a hormone that helps glucose (sugar) enter cells for energy. This means your body needs to produce more insulin to achieve the same effect, potentially leading to high blood sugar and increasing the risk of type 2 diabetes and other health problems. For midlife women struggling with insulin resistance is common during and after menopause.

Fasting can help restore insulin sensitivity, meaning our cells can readily absorb glucose (sugar) from the bloodstream, keeping blood sugar within a healthy range —making it easier to maintain a healthy weight and energy levels.

Enhancing Mental Clarity

Brain fog is one of the most frustrating symptoms of midlife. Intermittent Fasting stimulates the production of *brain-derived neurotrophic factor (BDNF)*—a protein that supports cognitive function, memory, and focus.

Activating Autophagy

During fasting, the body switches into repair mode, clearing out damaged cells and regenerating new ones through a process called **autophagy**. Think of it as your body's internal detox and anti-aging system.

Supporting Hormonal Balance

Fasting may help regulate key hormones like leptin (which controls hunger), and ghrelin (which signals fullness), helping you feel more in tune with your appetite and reducing emotional eating.

Promoting Fat Loss While Preserving Muscle

Unlike calorie restriction, Intermittent Fasting helps maintain lean muscle mass (especially when combined with protein-rich meals and resistance training)—crucial for strength, mobility, and metabolic health in midlife.

The Most Common Intermittent Fasting Protocols

There's no one-size-fits-all fasting method. And as midlife women, flexibility is our superpower. Here are the most popular styles of intermittent fasting:

12:12 Method

- **Eat:** Within a 12-hour window (e.g., 7am–7pm)
- **Fast:** 12 hours overnight

- **Great for:** Beginners or women with adrenal fatigue. Gentle and sustainable.

14:10 Method

- **Eat:** During a 10-hour window (e.g., 9am–7pm)
- **Fast:** For 14 hours overnight
- **Great for:** Supporting metabolic health without being too restrictive.

16:8 Method

- **Eat:** During an 8-hour window (e.g., 11am–7pm)
- **Fast:** For 16 hours overnight
- **Great for:** Women with weight loss goals and no signs of burnout or thyroid issues.

Each style can be effective—*the key is listening to your body, not following rigid rules.*

Why You Shouldn't Stick to the Same Fasting Routine Every Day

In Dr Mindy Pelz's wonderful book **"Fast Like a Girl"** she recommends that women especially those post-menopausal, mix up their fasting days. **Your body thrives on adaptation**. When you fast the same way every day, your metabolism can adjust *downward* to that predictable rhythm—potentially slowing weight loss or increasing fatigue.

Just like exercise, your fasting routine should be *cyclical*, not static.

How to Add Flexibility:

- **Mix it up weekly:** Do 12:12 on Monday, 14:10 midweek, and 16:8 a couple of days when you feel strong and energized.

- **Take fasting breaks:** On weekends or around your cycle (if still menstruating), loosen the fasting window or skip it entirely.

- **Pair with intuition:** If you're feeling exhausted, hungry, or anxious, it's okay to eat earlier. That's *wisdom*, not weakness.

Think of this like metabolic cross-training. The variation keeps your body responsive, your hormones happy, and your metabolism engaged.

Real Talk: What Intermittent Fasting Is *Not*

- It's not about skipping meals to "earn" food.

- It's not about punishing your body into submission.

- It's not a magic bullet that overrides poor nutrition, sleep, or stress.

It *is* a powerful tool. When used alongside intuitive eating, adequate protein, resistance training, and sleep—it becomes a cornerstone of midlife vitality.

When I first began experimenting with intermittent fasting, I approached it with curiosity, not control. Some days it felt amazing—other days I broke my fast early, guilt-free.

Over time, I noticed subtle shifts: more clarity in the morning, fewer sugar crashes, better digestion, deeper sleep.

It wasn't about being perfect. And I often reminded myself that Intermittent Fasting is a suggestion, not a religion. It was about *partnering* with my body instead of pushing it.

And in midlife, that partnership—between wisdom and science, between structure and softness—is the real power.

Reflection Prompts

- What fasting window feels most aligned with my current energy, stress levels, and lifestyle?

- How can I bring more flexibility and less rigidity to my wellness routine?

- On a scale from 1–10, how well am I tuning into my body's hunger and fullness cues?

- What stories do I hold about "not eating" that may no longer serve me?

- Where might intermittent fasting offer me more freedom, not more control?

Here are some **Myth-Busting Intermittent Fasting for Midlife Women**

Myth #1: "Fasting is just another diet."

Truth: Intermittent fasting isn't about restriction—it's about *rhythm*. It's not about what you eat, but *when* you eat. When practiced with flexibility, it can reduce the obsession with food and help you reconnect with real hunger cues.

Myth #2: "Women shouldn't fast—it messes with hormones."

Truth: Yes, if done aggressively or rigidly, fasting *can* disrupt hormones—especially for women under high stress or with thyroid/adrenal issues. But when done *gently and cyclically*, intermittent fasting supports hormone balance by improving insulin sensitivity, reducing inflammation, and promoting cellular repair.

Key: The fasting protocol must *fit the woman*, not the other way around.

Myth #3: "You need to do 16:8 or longer for results."

Truth: Longer isn't always better. Many midlife women thrive on 12:12 or 14:10 protocols. It's about consistency over time—not pushing yourself into deeper fasts you're not ready for.

Myth #4: "You'll lose muscle if you fast."

Truth: Muscle loss happens from *inactivity* and *undereating protein*—not from smart fasting. In fact, intermittent fasting *preserves* lean muscle mass when paired with adequate protein (100g/day or more) and resistance training.

Myth #5: "You have to fast every day."

Truth: The body thrives on variation. Fasting the same way every day can lead to metabolic adaptation (aka plateauing). Mix up your fasting windows. Take days off. Think *metabolic flexibility*, not monotony.

Myth #6: "Fasting slows your metabolism."

Truth: Chronic calorie restriction slows metabolism—not strategic fasting. In fact, Intermittent Fasting may support mitochondrial function and metabolic health by giving your digestive system a break and encouraging your body to use stored fat for fuel.

Myth #7: "You can eat anything during your eating window."

Truth: Technically, yes. But *nutritionally*, no. Fasting doesn't cancel out poor food choices. Whole foods, quality protein, healthy fats, and fiber-rich plants matter more than ever in midlife. Fasting *enhances* a nutrient-dense diet—it doesn't excuse a nutrient-lacking one.

Myth #8: "Fasting is just a trend."

Truth: Intermittent fasting is *ancient*. From spiritual practices to survival instincts, humans have fasted for centuries. Science is finally catching up to what many cultures have long known: periods of rest are just as essential as nourishment.

Final Word

You don't need to fast the way a 25-year-old biohacker does. You need to fast like a *wise*, evolving, intuitive midlife woman—someone who honors both science *and* self-awareness.

This is not about being perfect. It's about being in partnership with your body.

STRONG

Principle #3 - Exercise Effectively

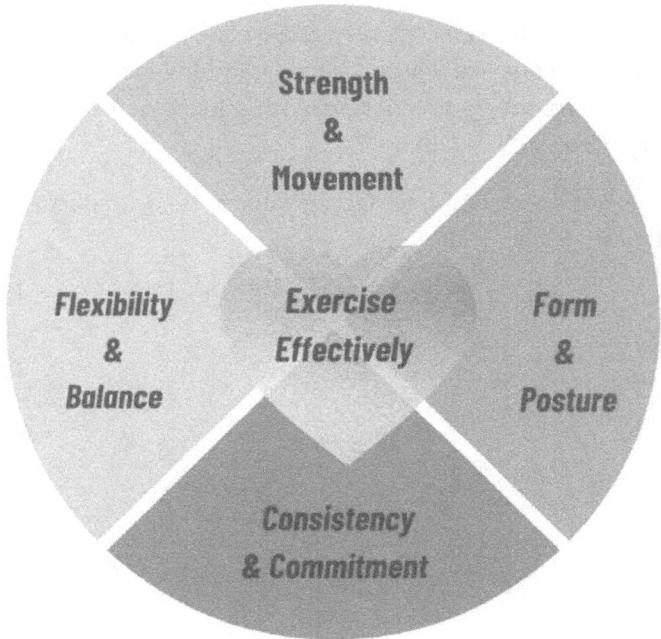

As I have mentioned in earlier chapters, my career began as a fitness instructor in the 1980's and since then, exercise has always been very important in my life.

In my 20's, I exercised many hours a day, and to be truthful, it had nothing to do with strength or energy, it was all about being able to eat more and stay skinny. That may work in your

20's, but not at all either practical or sustainable when you hit 50!

Many of us have been taught to move our bodies to shrink them. But by the time we reach midlife, our relationship with exercise has often become... complicated.

But in this next chapter of life, we don't move to punish—we move to **preserve, protect, and power up**. Exercise becomes a tool not just for fitness, but for long-term vitality, independence, and brain health.

When I was a young girl, every Monday in our house was laundry day. With five children to care for, it was an all-day effort. Mum would put the clothes in the washing machine, then take the heavy wet clothes out of the machine once the cycle was completed, run the clothes through a roller on top of the machine, to take all the water out, before putting them all back in the machine to rinse the clothes, the repeating the whole thing over again, before loading the clothes into the laundry basket and heading out to the line to hang them up to dry. This would be repeated maybe four to five times throughout the day. It was a very physical process.

When we first moved to Vancouver, I was doing the laundry one day and realised how easy the whole process was, compared to when my mother did laundry. In fact, the most amount of effort was putting the coins in the coin operated washing machine, before unloading the clothes from the washing machine into the dryer, right next to it!

Remember when you had to get out of your car to open your garage door, or you had to wind down the window of your car, using your arm, not your finger to push a button?

Or if you wanted to change the TV station, you had to get out of your chair and walk (heaven forbid) across the living room to the TV to physically change the channel? Can you imagine how your teenager would complain if they had to do that now?

It's as if every single normal thing we used to do, now has a simpler way of doing it, that involves less movement. But this lack of movement in the most normal day to day actions, is wreaking havoc on our bodies and our health.

Where generations ago, physical activity was an accepted way of life, these days convenience is. As I sit here and type this manuscript, I have to be very aware that I need to get up out of my chair every hour or so, to move my body. It could be so easy to sit here for hours and work, as many people in office jobs do.

The key? **Exercising Effectively**

Not just doing *more* but doing what matters, to support you now and into the future.

Effective movement in midlife focuses on **seven– essential pillars**:
Strength. Movement. Form. Posture. Flexibility. Balance. Consistency and Commitment

Let's break them down.

1. Strength – The Foundation of Functional Longevity

After 40, women lose muscle mass at a rate of three to eight percent per decade. After menopause, that loss accelerates. And this matters—because **muscle is protective**.

Muscle supports:

- **Metabolic health** – more muscle = better blood sugar control.
- **Bone density** – essential for avoiding osteoporosis.
- **Joint stability** – less risk of injury.

- **Immunity** – muscle plays a role in immune signaling.

And perhaps most importantly—it supports **mobility and independence** as we age. Strength training isn't just for aesthetics. It's an anti-aging, longevity, vitality tool. Quite simply your natural insurance policy to help you age well.

But strength training is more than just being about physical strength. A 2019 study in *Frontiers in Neuroscience* found that leg strength—specifically through movements like squats—correlates with **greater brain volume** and a reduced risk of neurodegenerative conditions such as Alzheimer's. Strong legs support better blood flow and neurological signaling between body and brain.

2. Movement – The Medicine of Midlife

We've been sold the myth that a single 30-minute workout can cancel out the damage of sitting for hours. But science tells a different story: it's not just about exercise; it's about *movement* throughout the day.

Regular daily movement supports:

- **Circulation and lymphatic flow** – helping the body detox naturally.
- **Blood sugar regulation** — movement after meals helps blunt glucose spikes.
- **Mood and mental clarity** — **movement** releases endorphins and regulates cortisol.
- **Joint lubrication and flexibility** — especially important as estrogen declines.
- **Energy and metabolism** — movement "wakes up" our cells and mitochondrial function.

And what's powerful is that movement doesn't have to mean exercise. By regularly incorporating short bursts of movement throughout your day can help power up your energy

A 2022 review in the *British Journal of Sports Medicine* found that even light-intensity movement accumulated throughout the day dramatically reduces risk of all-cause mortality, cardiovascular disease, and cognitive decline.

Movement is our midlife multivitamin. It fuels vitality, keeps our minds sharp, and reminds us that our bodies were made to *move*, not just perform.

7,000 Steps – The Science is In.

You've probably heard the magic number: 10,000 steps a day. While it originally began as a Japanese marketing idea to promote the original pedometer—a device that you attached to the laces of your shoes to count the steps you took, over time, studies have shown that 7,000 steps per day seems to be the ideal number for longevity and health. It's a surprisingly powerful, low-impact way to support almost every system in your body, especially in midlife.

Tracking steps is just a suggestion – not a religion! It is a way to help you become aware of increasing the number of times you move throughout the day. While the purpose of the magic number is to give you a goal to aim for, the real magic happens when you **spread those steps, or that incidental movement, throughout your day.**

Instead of one big walk and then hours of sitting, break your movement into short bursts.

- A 30-minute power walk first thing in the morning.
- A walk at lunchtime instead of sitting at your desk.

- Incorporate walking meetings during the day or instead of sending an email, walk to your colleague's desk!

- Park your car far from the entrance to the mall then walk fast through the shopping mall.

- If you catch public transport, walk to the next stop, instead of the closest one to you.

- If your Uber trip is less than 10 minutes away, turn that into a 35-minute walk.

- End your day with a 20-minute walk after dinner.

While adding extra steps to your day works in a perfect world, often due to weather or time constraints, they can be a challenge. Instead, you can add incidental movement that can also be of benefit.

- 10 power squats at your desk every hour, or after dinner.

- Challenge yourself (and your kids) to do push-ups between commercials on TV.

- While the kettle is waiting to boil, put on some music and dance for a couple of minutes.

Quite simply, when you focus on regularly moving your body, it all adds, up and gives your metabolism gentle nudges all day long, as well as managing blood sugar spikes, supporting digestion, and improving mood and focus.

Most importantly, increasing movement throughout the day reconnects you to **your body's rhythm**. We are not built to be sedentary, and yet our 21st century encourages it. Walk where you can and find ways to move your body. Movement helps boost your energy, your clarity and is your insurance against frailty.

The Power of Zone II Walking – Achievable Intensity. Profound Benefits.

We often think fitness means pushing hard—sweating, panting, going all out. But one of the most effective, sustainable, and science-backed forms of cardiovascular exercise doesn't leave you breathless.

It's called **Zone II Training**, and it's especially powerful for **midlife women.**

So, what is it?

Zone II refers to a **specific heart rate zone**—roughly **60 to 70 percent of your maximum heart rate**. It's the pace where:

- You can still **hold a conversation.**

- You're breathing more deeply, but not gasping.

- You feel **energized**, not exhausted.

In simple terms: **brisk walking** that feels comfortably challenging—but totally doable.

Why it Matters in Midlife

As estrogen declines in menopause, so does **mitochondrial efficiency**—your body's ability to turn food into energy.

Zone II Training **targets the mitochondria**, helping them work better, last longer, and multiply. This means:

- More energy throughout the day
- Improved fat metabolism
- Better blood sugar regulation
- Lower resting heart rate and blood pressure
- Reduced risk of cardiovascular disease
- Improved endurance and recovery

It's anti-aging, heart-protective, and hormone-supportive—all in one walk.

Your Brain Loves It Too

Zone II walking increases blood flow to the brain, supporting **memory, mental clarity, and emotional resilience**. It also reduces inflammation—one of the major drivers of brain aging.

Duration Matters More Than Intensity

The magic of Zone II is in the **time spent**, not the speed. Promise yourself to get at least 30 minutes three to five times per week. Even better if some of it is outdoors at sunrise or sunset.

The Power of HIIT

And there is a way to make your walk even more beneficial, and that is by adding a few, 20-second High Intensity Interval Training (HIIT) bursts of energy to your walk.

HIIT has been used in training athletes for years, it means adding 20 second higher intensity bursts at various intervals to your normal workout.

What is exciting is that there is some research to show that HIIT has several great anti-aging and health benefits.

It has been shown to help lengthen our telomeres, which are best described as like little caps that sit on the end of your chromosomes. As we age, our telomeres shorten and that can lead to premature cellular ageing.

In addition to affecting telomeres, the wide variety of anti-aging HIIT benefits include:

- Firmer skin/less wrinkles
- Increased energy

- Boosted metabolism
- Improved libido
- Muscle tone improvement
- Reduced body fat

It has also been known to improve the function of those two pesky hormones ghrelin and leptin, mediating long-term regulation of energy balance and suppresses food intake, thereby inducing weight loss.

So, what would it look like? As an example, on a 30-minute Zonell Walk (fast enough to feel your heart pumping, but also able to carry on a conversation) add three 20-second bursts of walking as fast as you can, I can guarantee you will feel the energy benefits for hours after.

Walk with the Sun – The Healing Power of Light at Sunrise and Sunset

There's a quiet magic in walking under the early morning or late evening sky. Not just for the beauty, or the peace—but because **sunlight itself is medicine**, especially in midlife.

When you step outside at sunrise and sunset, you expose your eyes to **low-angle, full-spectrum light**—and this does something extraordinary: It resets your internal clock (circadian rhythm)

Early morning sunlight signals your brain to wake up, while increasing serotonin, your body's natural feel-good hormone. Then at dusk, helps your body create melatonin, the natural sleep hormone.

This natural rhythm supports:

- Deeper, more restorative sleep

- Improved hormone regulation (especially cortisol and melatonin)
- Better mood and sharper focus during the day

Why without sunglasses?

During these specific windows (within the first hour after sunrise and last hour before sunset), the UV index is low, and the sunlight is gentle.

By exposing your eyes—without lenses or filters—you allow your **retina** to absorb natural light signals. This stimulates the **suprachiasmatic nucleus**, the part of your brain that controls your body's master clock.

(Important: You're not staring *into* the sun—just being outside, facing natural light.)

Midlife, Melatonin, and Light

As we age, our **natural melatonin production decreases**, and poor sleep becomes more common. Walking at sunrise and sunset is a simple, potent way to signal the body to *make more of what it's missing.*

And walking itself—at these liminal times of day—adds a layer of soul nourishment. It becomes a **ritual**, not just a routine.

A chance to:

Set intentions before the world wakes up

- Reflect and release at the end of the day
- Reconnect to nature's rhythm—and your own

The Benefits of Walking After Dinner

A simple walk after dinner can be one of the most powerful yet overlooked habits for midlife health. Just 10 - 20 minutes of movement after your evening meal helps your body manage blood sugar more efficiently by improving insulin sensitivity. When you walk, your muscles actively use glucose for energy, which helps lower blood sugar levels and reduces the post-meal insulin spike. Over time, this can lead to better metabolic flexibility—meaning your body becomes more efficient at switching between burning carbohydrates and fat for fuel. For midlife women, this matters more than ever. As estrogen levels decline, insulin resistance often increases, making it easier to gain weight and harder to lose it—especially around the belly. Evening walks counteract this by reducing glucose buildup in the bloodstream and encouraging your cells to respond more effectively to insulin. The result? Better energy, less inflammation, improved fat metabolism, and a gentler transition through menopause. It's a small, sustainable habit that delivers big returns—physically and mentally.

Form & Posture– The Art of Moving Well

At midlife, it's not just about moving it's about moving with purpose!

Proper form helps:

- Align joints to reduce wear and tear
- Strengthen postural muscles to combat the "slouch" of sitting and stress
- Prevent injuries and overuse strain
- Create efficiency in movement

Form isn't about perfection. It's about awareness. Mindful movement teaches us to *listen* to our bodies—not override them. When we prioritize form over force, we can reduce injury and feel stronger in everyday life.

Good form also helps improve posture. And honestly, nothing ages us faster than poor posture. Now as we spend much of our day at a desk on a computer, our posture can suffer.

With every single exercise you do, see if you can watch yourself in the mirror. Standing tall, shoulders down and back, engage your abdominal muscles, tuck your hips slightly under and with each exercise ensure you are doing full range of motion. Catch the reflection of yourself in the windows of the stores at the mall, what does your posture look like? While you are sitting, sit up straight, engage and lift up through your core drop your shoulders and straighten your back (you are doing it now aren't you ☺). It is those small awarenesses every now and then that will make all the difference to your posture and help your energy flow through your body!

Flexibility & Balance – The Key to Ageless Grace

We often associate flexibility with yoga poses or touching our toes, but flexibility is more than that. As we age, connective tissues become stiffer, and joints lose range of motion. Tight muscles can:

- Increase fall risk
- Limit mobility
- Lead to compensatory movement patterns (and pain)

Gentle stretching and mobility work. especially in the hips, hamstrings, and shoulders—restore ease. Flexibility helps us *feel younger* in our bodies. Include stretching in your workouts, both before and after. And stand up and stretch regularly throughout the day to feel more aligned and less stuck physically and emotionally!

Balance – A Superpower for the Body *and* Brain

Balance isn't just about staying upright. It's a **neurological process**—a sign that your brain, inner ear, eyes, and muscles are communicating well.

With age, balance naturally declines. That's why incorporating simple balance drills—like standing on one foot, can significantly reduce the risk of falls, which remain a major cause of injury in women over 50.

But balance training goes beyond safety. It stimulates the brain.

A 2022 study in *Nature Scientific Reports* showed that balance exercises activate the **cerebellum and prefrontal cortex**—areas related to memory, planning, and focus. Regular balance training may help maintain mental clarity and cognitive flexibility as we age.

Incorporate balance training daily. While you are standing at the kitchen sink, waiting for the kettle to boil, stand on one leg, right first then left. Once you have mastered that, do the same thing with your eyes closed! Include balance work after EVERY workout.

Below is an indication of the number of seconds you should be able to balance, according to your age.

Eyes Open	Eyes Closed
Age 40 – 40 seconds seconds	Age 40 – 13
Age 50 – 41 seconds seconds	Age 50 – 8
Age 60 - 32 seconds seconds	Age 60 – 4

Age 70 and up – 10 – 14 seconds   Age 70 and up
– 3 seconds

6. Consistency and Commitment – The Secret Ingredient

Our new mid-life mantra needs to reflect the change in our mind and body.

Strong over Skinny

Health over Weight

Consistency over Intensity

Commitment over Measurement

Focus on the big picture – the long-term game, instead of sporadic short-term results. Your body is different now. You are not going to get results from a six-week fitness challenge, like you used to get when you were 20. Your commitment to consistent movement and two to three strength workouts a week, done with presence, purpose, and patience, focusing on your longevity, will outperform any sporadic 'fitness sprint.' Your body responds to regular input, not random bursts.

In midlife, we stop chasing burnout and start building momentum. Movement becomes a non-negotiable part of *who we are*—not something we do to fix ourselves. Commit to challenging yourself to master and increase weights on simple, compound muscle moves, such squats, lunges, push-ups, planks etc. Mastering each exercise, performed with correct form, but increasing weight over time, gives you such a sense of accomplishment and confidence.

The Nine Minute Workout

Several years ago, I broke a bone in my foot. Walking fast and trying to pass another slower walker, I stepped off the sidewalk and into a hole where the grass meets the concrete.

I fractured the fifth Metatarsal. A bone that my orthopaedic surgeon kindly nicknamed 'the dancer's fracture, it sounded so much nicer than an 'old lady fracture.'

While no surgery was required, I was forced to wear a boot for six weeks. I was devastated. We were in Covid lockdown, so gyms were closed. My daily walks had kept me sane!

One day, feeling very sorry for myself, I was googling for some solutions, when I came across some evidence about the 7-Minute Workout and the combination of certain exercises done over a short period of time, could be just as beneficial as a 30-minute workout.

The more I researched, the more my fitness professional mind started creating ideas. And over time, the 9-Minute workout was born.

It has evolved over the years (considering the first workouts were done with a boot) and now has become my favorite routine whenever I am pushed for time or in between gym workouts.

These workouts combine all the pillars of exercising purposefully – Strength, HIIT, Form, Flexibility and Balance. As well as some light jumping, which has been shown to improve bone health.

To download your free 9-Minute workout series, and the various variations as a companion to this book - click here
https://www.9minworkout/rego

Sally Thibault

Strong

Principle #4: Sleep Soundly

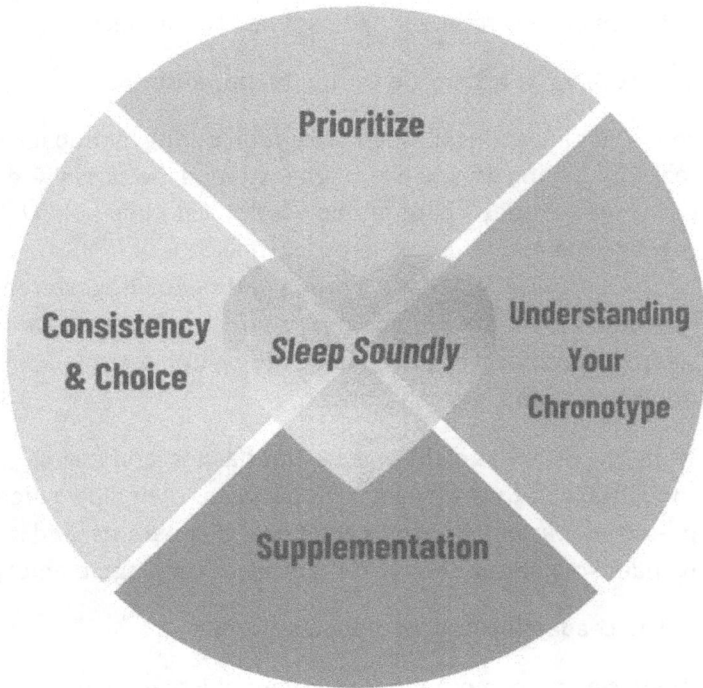

It's 2am. Again.

You've woken up for what feels like the hundredth night in a row—your body's tired, but your mind is racing. You're cycling through to-do lists, hormonal surges, flashes of heat, waves of worry or reliving every perceived mistake or interaction in your life since you were 16. The sun rises and you're left exhausted, frustrated, and wondering, "How am I supposed to lead like this?"

If this feels familiar, you're not alone. Sleep disturbances are one of the most common and frustrating challenges of the menopausal transition. And yet, many midlife women are told it's "just part of aging" or "a stage to get through." It's not. Prioritizing the quality of your sleep is an important as nutrition and exercise during this time of your life.

1. Why Sleep Is a Struggle During Menopause

You're not imagining it, sleep disruption during menopause is real. Fluctuating estrogen and progesterone levels can wreak havoc on the body's natural sleep cycles. Estrogen helps regulate the body's use of serotonin and other neurotransmitters that affect mood and sleep. Progesterone has a natural sedative effect, promoting deep, restorative sleep. As both decline, sleep becomes lighter, more fragmented, and less restorative.

Then there are the **night sweats**, **hot flashes**, and **racing thoughts**. Add to that the emotional stress of midlife: career pressures, parenting teens, caring for aging parents, and it's no wonder so many women find themselves running on empty.

2. The Leadership Cost of Sleepless Nights

When sleep is compromised so is your ability to lead. Interrupted sleep increases cortisol (the body's stress hormone) and can heighten anxiety, reduce emotional resilience, and impair decision-making. This isn't just inconvenient. For women in leadership roles, it's a silent saboteur.

Poor sleep affects:

- **Emotional regulation**—making it harder to stay grounded in high-pressure situations

- **Cognitive clarity**—impacting focus, memory, and innovative thinking
- **Confidence**—the mental fog and irritability erode the strong, clear, unapologetic voice you've worked so hard to embody.

In midlife, many women report feeling like they're 'losing their edge.' But what they're often losing... is sleep.

3. Sleep and Your Metabolism: The Hidden Link

Beyond brain fog, poor sleep has a direct impact on metabolism and fat storage. When you don't sleep deeply:

- **Insulin sensitivity decreases**—making your body more likely to store fat (especially around the belly).
- **Hunger hormones Ghrelin and Leptin rise**—which means you crave more food but feel less full.
- **Cortisol remains elevated**—encouraging fat storage and muscle breakdown.
- **The body becomes less efficient at recovering from workouts**—diminishing the results of even your most intentional fitness efforts.

You can eat well, train smart, and supplement but without good sleep, your body can't do the healing work that leads to fat loss and strength gain. In fact, as Dr. Bill Campbell, a leading researcher into fat loss has found in his latest research into menopause and fat loss says, *"Quite simply if you are not sleeping well, you cannot lose fat."*

4. Sleep, Brain health & Longevity

Emerging research shows that poor sleep in midlife is not just an inconvenience—it can impact our long-term brain health.

For years, scientists have looked at the connection between sleep and Alzheimer's disease. In 2023, researchers with the

University of California, Berkeley, published a study finding deep sleep is "almost like a life raft that keeps memory afloat" because it can mitigate the impacts from excessive deposits of beta-amyloid (a protein in the brain linked to memory loss caused by dementia).

Additionally, consistent sleep of seven to nine hours per night has been linked to greater longevity, stronger immune function, and improved cellular repair. In essence, sleep is not a passive state, it is one of the most powerful regenerative tools we have for preserving memory, clarity, and vitality as we age.

So, let's look at some solutions, first acknowledging where you are at now, and identifying your sleep chronotype.

Sleep Audit: Reclaiming Your Nighttime Power

Use this audit to reflect honestly on your current sleep habits. Rate each statement below from 1 (Rarely/Never) to 5 (Always).

Statement

___I fall asleep easily within 20 minutes.

___I stay asleep through the night without waking up.

___I wake feeling refreshed and energized.

___I go to bed and wake at roughly the same time each day.

___I avoid screens (TV/phone) for at least 1 hour before bed.

___My bedroom is dark, quiet, and cool.

___I don't consume caffeine after 2pm.

___I feel clear-headed and emotionally steady during the day.

___I rarely need naps or extra caffeine to function.

___I move my body during the day to support good sleep.

Total Score: _____ / 50

Interpretation:

- **40–50:** Your sleep habits are strong. Keep honouring your nighttime rhythm.

- **30–39:** You're doing well, but small shifts could lead to deeper rest.

- **20–29:** Sleep may be affecting your energy, metabolism, or mental clarity.

- **Below 20:** Time to reclaim your sleep - and your power. Start with one or two habits to support you.

What's Your Sleep Chronotype?

I came across this concept of sleep chronotypes after reading Dr. Micheal Brues's fabulous book, *The Power of When*.

I am an 'early riser, early to bed' gal. I usually wake naturally between 5 and 5:30am, I will only ever workout in the morning and have boundless energy until around lunchtime—but don't ask me to go anywhere or engage in deep meaningful conversations after 9pm!

Gerry is totally opposite. He goes to bed late and wakes usually around 7am. He will sit up for hours at night, often deep in thought or watching a movie. I have learned over the years that I am best not to ask him important questions until after his morning coffee and he prefers to exercise at night.

After reading *The Power of When,* I was able to better understand why certain routines work for some and not others, and at the same time, serve my clients in helping them create sleep, exercise and work routines.

Our chronotype determines the best time to sleep, wake, work, move, and even eat. Answer the questions below to discover your dominant rhythm.

1. How do you feel waking up in the morning (without an alarm)?

- A) Alert and ready to go

- B) Sleepy, but fine within 30 minutes

- C) Groggy and irritable - don't talk to me

- D) Anxious or restless - already thinking ahead

2. When are you most productive?

- A) Early morning

- B) Mid-morning to early afternoon

- C) Late afternoon to evening

- D) All over the place - hard to find a groove

3. Which best describes your sleep patterns?

- A) Fall asleep early, wake up early

- B) Typical 10pm – 6pm or 11pm – 7am sleeper

- C) Stay up late, struggle with mornings

- D) Light sleeper, toss and turn often

4. Your ideal time for exercise is:

- A) Before 8am

- B) Mid-morning or lunchtime

- C) After 5pm

- D) I find it hard to be consistent

5. How do you handle stress or deadlines?

- A) I plan ahead and get it done early

- B) I work steadily and manage it well

- C) I procrastinate but thrive under pressure

- D) I get overwhelmed and struggle to focus

Your Results:

Count your most frequent letter:

- **Mostly A: You're a *Lion***
  Energetic in the morning but tend to crash by evening. Your best work happens before noon. Bedtime by 9-10pm works best.

- **Mostly B: You're a *Bear***
  You follow the rhythm of the sun and represent 50-55 per cent of people. Seven–eight hours of sleep, regular routines, and mid-morning productivity suit you.

- **Mostly C: You're a *Wolf***
  Creative, intuitive night owl. Your energy peaks later in the day. Protect your slow mornings, and don't force early routines.

- **Mostly D: You're a *Dolphin***
  Light sleeper, often anxious or sensitive to routine.

Sleep hygiene and nervous system regulation are essential for you.

Knowing your chronotype is not about limitation, it's about understanding. You don't need to force yourself into someone else's rhythm. Midlife is the perfect time to align with your natural flow. Go to www.thesleepdoctor.com for more information about your sleep type.

5. The Ritual of Rest: Routines That Restore

Creating a bedtime ritual is one of the most underestimated leadership strategies for midlife women. It's not about perfection - it's about **choice and consistency.**

Create a wind-down routine to prioritize your bedtime before you want to actually be asleep, not when you want to go to bed. Some techniques include:

- No alcohol or sweet foods at least two hours before bed.

- Turn your phone to sleep mode and leave to charge outside of the bedroom 90 minutes before you want to go to sleep.

- Tidy the living room and kitchen *(it's amazing how good you feel when your living area is cleared of clutter before you go to bed!)*

- Turn off all bright lights in the kitchen and living room.

- Take magnesium or any night-time supplements to help with sleep.

- Write out your 'to do' list for the next day, it helps your brain relax.

- Lay out your workout clothes or clothes for the next day so you don't have to think about it in the morning.

- Take time with your nighttime skin routine, cleansing your face and massaging your moisturizer into your skin can help you feel relaxed.

- Make sure your room is fairly cool and, where possible, use black out curtains or a sleep mask.

- Invest in a silk pillowcase. They can help keep your head and neck cool throughout the night and are great for your skin and hair.

- Read at least a few pages of a 'real' book before you go to sleep.

- Inhale essential oils such as lavender, chamomile, bergamot or sandalwood—they can help release stress and promote a calm mind.

- Practise 4-4-8 deep breathing: Breath in for the count of four, hold for the count of four, and exhale for the count of eight. While you are doing this, ensure that you are taking deep breaths and consciously relaxing your body at the same time. Be mindful of anywhere you are holding tension

Think of a sleep routine as the bodies nightly reset. Don't treat rest as a luxury; it's your most reliable investment in a longer, healthier life.

6. Supplements That Can Support Deep Sleep

While supplements aren't a cure-all, they can gently support the body's natural sleep processes—especially during hormonal transitions.

Some sleep-supportive supplements include:

- **Magnesium (especially glycinate or threonate):** Calms the nervous system and supports GABA production
- **Saffron:** reduces stress, and positively influences the body's sleep-regulating hormone melatonin & cortisol
- **L-Theanine:** Reduces anxiety and promotes relaxation
- **GABA:** The body's natural calming neurotransmitter
- **Melatonin:** Best used short-term or in microdoses (.3mg–1mg) to reset circadian rhythms
- **Ashwagandha:** Helps reduce cortisol and support adrenal function
- **Valerian Root or Passionflower:** Traditionally used for calming and sleep.

Always consult your health practitioner, especially if you're on medications or managing health conditions.

7. Eating Your Way to Good Sleep

Tryptophan is an essential amino acid that the body cannot produce, so it must be obtained through food. It is used to create proteins, as well as important compounds to help you sleep, like the neurotransmitter serotonin, the hormone melatonin, and vitamin B3 (niacin).

Some foods that are ideal to help promote sleep include:

- **Meat and Poultry:** Turkey, chicken, lamb shoulder
- **Fish:** Lobster, octopus, crab, salmon, and other types of fish
- **Dairy:** Cheddar cheese, parmesan cheese, milk, and cottage cheese
- **Eggs:** A single egg contains a significant amount of tryptophan
- **Nuts and Seeds:** Pumpkin seeds, sunflower seeds, chia seeds, and sesame seeds

- **Legumes:** Soybeans, tofu, and tempeh
- **Grains:** Wheat germ and oat bran
- **Fruits:** Cherries (especially tart cherry juice), bananas pineapple, Kiwi fruit & Avocado

Foods that May Disrupt Sleep Quality

While some foods help promote a good night's sleep others can interfere, especially during menopause when the hormonal changes also impact on the health of your gut microbiome.

Foods that may disrupt sleep:

- **Caffeine:** Found in coffee, tea, chocolate, and soda drinks. It is a stimulant that blocks adenosine, a sleep-promoting chemical

- **High-fat and greasy foods:** Fried items, fatty meats, and pizza can cause indigestion and acid reflux, making it harder to sleep

- **Spicy foods:** Can lead to heartburn and discomfort, especially in people prone to acid reflux

- **Acidic foods:** Citrus fruits and tomatoes can also trigger indigestion

- **Alcohol:** While it may initially cause drowsiness, it disrupts REM sleep and decreases overall sleep quality

- **Sugary snacks and refined carbs:** These can cause blood sugar spikes and subsequent crashes (especially at 2am!) which may disturb sleep

- **Processed meats:** High in sodium and unhealthy fats, they can interfere with sleep

As with all things, these lists are a suggestion—not a religion. I certainly don't follow all these rules every night, and, realistically, neither will you. But if you are aware of strong, empowered choices *most of the time*, you can adjust and understand what the cause of some sleep problems may be. This is adopting self-leadership and being empowered, not a victim to your circumstances.

Sleep Is Not a Luxury - It's a Leadership Tool

In midlife, your sleep must become a sacred ritual, placing just as much importance on it as you do exercise or nutrition.

Sleep is not something to *fight through* or *patch over* with caffeine and grit. It's an investment in your future - one that allows you to rise each day strong, clear, and unapologetically you.

CLEAR

Principle #5: Process Emotion Consciously

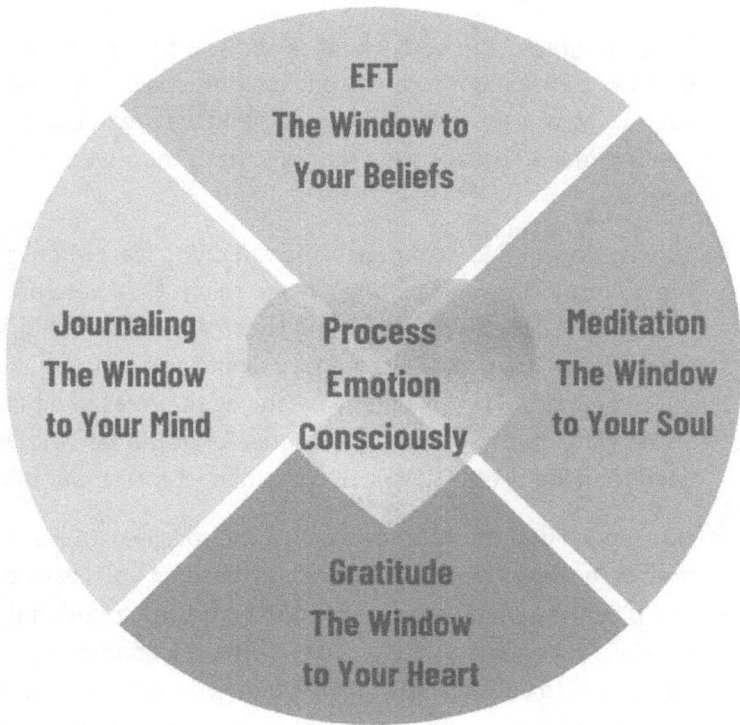

EFT
The Window to
Your Beliefs

Journaling
The Window
to Your Mind

Process
Emotion
Consciously

Meditation
The Window
to Your Soul

Gratitude
The Window
to Your Heart

The journey to become strong, clear and unapologetic in your life and leadership is just that: a journey. It's not outside of you, but rather, within.

In my experience, menopause highlights almost every single negative thought or limiting belief you have ever had. It's like the protective filter in your brain suddenly disappears, replaced by feelings of uncertainty, anxiety, low self-worth.

Research has highlighted an increased risk in anxiety, depression and suicidal ideation, especially in perimenopause, for many women. In generations before us, women were often diagnosed with 'hysteria', or called whiney women, their symptoms referred to being all in the mind.

But as our brain and body changes, it's as if the armour we could so easily and effectively pull on in the past to ensure that everything was as normal, falls away, and we are left with feelings of inadequacy and emotions that simply were hidden before.

So how do you find confidence and energy to lead when it feels like your priorities are shifting? When things that were once important, suddenly seem insignificant? When your daily *To Do* list seems to never end, leaving you exhausted and overwhelmed. When suddenly balancing the roles of daughter, sister, wife, mother, friend, and professional woman, that you used to manage effortlessly, become almost insurmountable?

How do we find the courage to be authentically who we really are when some days it's easier to silence what you really think and play the game, because you don't have the emotional bandwidth to keep up the facade? When rejection or challenges to your leadership create emotions, you are not used to or have always ignored, but now send you into a deep, dark spiral that makes you question if you have just 'lost it'?

Now it's time for the deeper questions combined with more thoughtful responses.

On this unapologetic leadership journey, there are no judgments—only choices. When I am working with clients or facilitating a menopause in the workplace workshop, I begin by asking one question, "What do you **really** want?"

What is extraordinary is that so many midlife women have the same answer - *"I thought I knew—but now I am not so sure"*.

That uncertainty comes from years, decades even, of handing our power over to others to make decisions for us or choosing to conform to our peer or friendship groups, rather than speaking up and risk being alienated or isolated. We played by the rules; Didn't speak up at meetings so we wouldn't upset the corporate apple cart or, trusted someone else's rules, instead of trusting ourselves.

In this menopause transition, that changes. It's like a universal collective pulse. As our brain changes with our fluctuating hormones, we start to question what's real for us. We simply want to rediscover our own power and let go of the issues that no longer serve us, because we lose that filter that has previously kept us safe. It's unnerving in the beginning, not only for you, but for those around you who have been used to you going along with what they think.

Now is the time to make the best choices *for yourself* from the greatest expression *of* yourself—when you know who you are, and what you really want. In that order.

No Judgements - Just Choices

On this unapologetic leadership journey, there are no judgments—only choices.

Becoming the authentic leader, you were born to be, only happens when you commit to reclaiming all the lost, hurt, sad, and frightened aspects of yourself—and healing them.

You are not separate from your body, and your body is not a machine operating independently from your heart and mind. Every part of your life reflects your past experiences:

- All those experiences you pretended to ignore, but deep down they hurt.

- All the times you were overlooked, shouted at, bullied, or teased.

- All the times you wanted to be seen, noticed, loved, or accepted but felt left out.

- All the times you felt you were never as pretty, thin, or popular as the "cool girls".

All of it still lives in you.

That little 4-year-old or 16-year-old version of you, still carries her pain. It may look different now, but unless you've truly healed, it's still yours. I can't tell you how many clients have said to me, *"Oh, that happened years ago. I've moved on."*

My response? No, you haven't.

How do I know?

Because it still shows up, without fail, in one (or all) of these three areas:

- Your body
- Your relationships
- Your bank account

Most people I work with, might have one of those areas of their life handled, but the other two are a struggle. And sometimes, it's all three.

Want to know if you're really over that thing that happened years ago? Look there. If one of those areas evokes even the smallest emotional response, then you haven't resolved it, you've buried it.

When we don't honour our emotions,

we become confused by them.

Instead of feeling the sadness of a father who was never there, we lash out at our partner because he doesn't hear us.

Instead of feeling the sting of exclusion from the cool group in school, we work longer hours, chasing perfection and overachievement, hoping we are noticed this time!

Instead of feeling the pain of never being acknowledged by our parents, we numb ourselves with food, alcohol, or scrolling social media.

Every past pain and unresolved emotion still exists within you, and it will continue to weigh you down until you remove its emotional charge.

Every emotion you feel now has a root cause. It started somewhere. You can't change the memory, but you *can* change the trigger.

When something from your past hasn't been processed, it triggers an emotional response. How you react depends on how emotionally free you are.

Look out for feelings or words such as:

"It always happens to me."
"There's nothing I can do to change this."
"This is just the way it is."

These statements are not true.

Nothing is ever 'just the way it is' If it were, we'd still be riding in wagons and lighting candles to see in the dark. History only moves forward because someone believes, 'there has to be a better way'.

And that's true for you too.

We do what we do, based on what we know. Repeating patterns are just that –*patterns* – rooted in a belief and charged with emotion from a past experience. But when we know better, we do better.

But until then, those emotions stay trapped in your body, your relationships, your finances. And they feel heavy. They dim your light. They slow you down.

But once you release them? A lightness returns.

A client who was six weeks into her six-month coaching journey told me, *"People keep saying I look amazing and asking if I've lost weight. I haven't. But I just feel lighter."*

That's the power of release. When you let go of the emotions you've been holding onto, when you reframe pain into wisdom, it is unbelievably freeing. Others can see it. They notice the joy on your face, the ease in your posture, the calm in your voice.

This unapologetic leadership journey is, at its core, a journey back to *you*.

Imagine what it would feel like to trust your intuition without question; To know that your wisdom flows through you with grace; To wake up each day in a life that feels aligned and true.

That's what these midlife years, *all 50+ of them*, are meant to be.

Speeding Up the Process

When I began this journey, I did it the hard way.

I had no idea about neuroplasticity or that you could change behaviour, by changing beliefs using tools that we now know so much more about. Instead, I relied on a simple and time-consuming approach: repeating affirmations over and over again.

But 30 years later, there's a wealth of knowledge available. Practices such as meditation, Emotional Freedom Techniques (Tapping), Neurolinguistic Programming (NLP), Hypnotherapy, Breathwork, visualisation, journaling, and gratitude help us fast-track the transformation process.

In my experience, this midlife leadership journey isn't just about *mindset*. I prefer to think of this as a *belief-set* journey—creating a powerful belief-set that aligns with the authenticity of you. What is the point of forcing your mind to think something if your past stories trigger you every time to try to step outside your brain's comfort zone?

But this all takes time.

In his bestselling book *Atomic Habits*, author James Clear cites research showing it can take up to 66 days to move from willpower-based decision making to an actual habit. Sixty-six days of pushing through discomfort and resisting the pull to quit.

Why so long? Because our brain is hardwired to keep us safe. It wants to make sense of the world by locking in what we believe to be true, and it doesn't like change or uncertainty. But if you're serious about this journey, those are two things you'll have to get used to. We're so accustomed to instant gratification that we forget all change happens on *its* timeline, not ours.

Over the past year, we've had the absolute joy of caring for a couple of my daughter's friends' babies. When we moved to Vancouver we gained not only honorary kids, but a couple of honorary grandchildren, too. And honestly, nothing fills my heart more than taking care of these tiny humans (and then handing them back!).

Since we're not their biological grandparents it's often a few weeks between visits, but every time we see them, I'm in awe of how much they've changed. From completely dependent to sitting up, crawling, and courageously attempting those first wobbly steps.

And every time, I watch the determination on their tiny faces as they reach for something just out of their grasp; or keep falling over when they are trying to master the art of walking. But they don't give up, they just keep doing it repeatedly, gaining more confidence and more ability each time

And I often wonder: When did *we* lose that?

When did willpower and determination become something, we judged ourselves for not having, when we didn't get it right on the first try? The first step to change is making the decision. Then comes the 66 days of grace and patience for yourself. Both require energy. In the beginning, a lot of it. Until your new choice becomes second nature, you'll need to believe in the process and speak kindly (and occasionally firmly) to yourself to stay on track.

When I worked as a fitness instructor, the biggest challenge we faced wasn't getting people to sign up, it was keeping them motivated.

At the start of a weight loss or fitness program, people were always excited and full of determination. The more they paid, the more committed they seemed. For the first two weeks, they'd show up early for class, hit the treadmill or rower before we even began class, and talked enthusiastically about their new eating plan.

But by week three, things started to shift. Muscles ached, nutrition discipline wavered, excuses crept in. That's when, as instructors, we knew we had to pivot. Our focus moved from exercise and nutrition to *commitment* and *motivation*. By week five, many began skipping classes or turning up on Monday saying, *"I totally blew it on the weekend, but I'm back on track today!"*

We were in no-man's land. That delicate space where doubt kicks in, motivation dips, old beliefs bubble up, and past patterns try to reclaim control. Now that I understand what was happening, beneath the surface, I see it clearly: it was the space where patience and belief were most needed, because the new habit hadn't quite cemented yet.

Thankfully, today we have better tools. Tools that make those 66 days less of a grind and more of a supported path. Tools that harness the brain's power *for* change, not against it. And the first of those tools is a modality that was once relatively unknown but is now, thanks to research and media, gaining traction fast.

Tool #1 Emotional Freedom Technique – The Window to Your Beliefs

As mentioned in Principle #1, Emotional Freedom Techniques (EFT/Tapping) has been one of the most powerful modalities in my life. It completely transformed not only how I viewed food and my body, but also how I viewed myself.

EFT blends modern psychology and acupressure, using gentle tapping on meridian points on the face and upper body while verbalising how you're feeling. Once mastered, it's easy to do whenever you're feeling stressed or anxious. It has been documented to reduce cortisol so you can think with greater clarity and connect more deeply with your intuition and wisdom.

Now widely practised, EFT has been the subject of over 100 clinical trials and peer-reviewed studies. It's shown to be effective not just for stress, but also for phobias (like fear of flying or heights), anxiety, depression, PTSD, physical pain, food cravings, and more.

When I began tapping daily, the lightness I felt in my body and mind was extraordinary. Many of my clients describe the same experience after a session, often saying, "I feel so much lighter."

When you release the weight of limiting beliefs, you feel more energy, more vitality. Your intuition becomes clearer, and your inner wisdom begins to flow. EFT opens the path to understanding why we hold ourselves back with limiting stories about our capabilities.

If you haven't experienced EFT before, please refer to the appendix at the back of this book or check out my YouTube Channel for follow-along tapping videos.

Tool #2 Meditation - The Window to Your Soul

"You should sit in meditation for 20 minutes a day.
Unless you're too busy, then you should sit for an hour."
- Zen Proverb

Of all four tools, this one was the most difficult for me to adopt but it's now non-negotiable. I start every day with meditation. It grounds me and makes everything flow more smoothly.

While meditation and mindfulness are ancient practices, we now have a wealth of research to back up their benefits. In a *Scientific American* article, author Tom Ireland outlines how meditation affects the brain, specifically, the amygdala which governs fear and emotion. Meditation helps shrink the amygdala while strengthening the prefrontal cortex, the area responsible for clear thinking, focus, and decision-making.

The website *Headspace*, one of the largest platforms for meditation, currently hosts over 65 ongoing studies exploring the effects of meditation.

My favourite meditation practice is led by Dr. Joe Dispenza. His work focuses on aligning with your body's emotions—a vital part of learning to trust your intuition and inner guidance. One of his phrases during a morning meditation is: *"Can you teach your body emotionally what it feels like...?"* YES. That's the goal. To truly feel the emotion in your body and trust it.

This was the greatest challenge for me when I first started meditating. I thought meditation meant silencing my thoughts, and I struggled with that. But after doing one of Dr. Joe's meditations for maybe the hundredth time, I finally got it.

It's not about *stillness* of the mind; it's about *connection* to the body.

Like EFT, meditation helps you *feel* what's going on inside your body—your stress, your joy, your fear, your anger—and teaches you to recognise those emotions as signals, not threats.

Emotions are felt in your body, for example, excitement in the belly, love in the heart, stress in your shoulders, anger in your hands, headaches when you're overwhelmed. These sensations are physical manifestations of feelings not yet resolved.

During this menopausal transition and our mid-life leadership journey, it is really empowering to re-learn how to identify, feel, and release emotions. Why? Because amid the brain fog, hot flashes, sleepless nights, and anxiety, our emotions can be all over the place, causing more stress, often making those symptoms worse.

Maybe it will be the first time you have done this in a long time, if at all. But you are in the most powerful time of your life. You are literally reimagining your midlife years and how you want to show up. You are not separate from your body. As a feminine leader, learning to feel again is your superpower.

I once worked with a client who was constantly dealing with workplace drama. She was exhausted and frustrated, always putting out fires. Through coaching, she uncovered a pattern that reflected her childhood. Her mother yelled a lot, and as a sensitive child, the yelling made her feel anxious and stressed. It was a feeling she carried through to her leadership—always feeling responsible to fix everybody else's issues.

She began incorporating a 20-minute daily meditation practice and found it really served her throughout the day. Whenever an issue between her team members arose, she found, over time, that she could easily shift into breathing deeply and calming her mind, which allowed her to observe the drama from a different perspective and as she said, *"It gave me more clarity and a sense of order and peace. I felt really comfortable in being able to remove myself emotionally from the drama, and watch it, without buying into it."*

While meditation is good for your soul, did you know it is also a great longevity tool and may slow down biological ageing?

Research shows regular meditation can:

1. **Reduce stress, lower inflammation, and improve sleep** – all key factors linked to accelerated aging. Chronic stress floods the body with cortisol, which can contribute to inflammation and poor sleep.

2. **Increase telomerase activity** - A landmark study led by Australian Nobel Prize–winning scientist Dr. Elizabeth Blackburn found that meditation and mindfulness practices can increase telomerase activity (the enzyme responsible for maintaining and even lengthening telomeres) thereby supporting cellular repair and longevity *(Epel et al., Annals of the New York Academy of Sciences, 2009)*.

3. **Strengthen the brain** - MRI studies reveal long-term meditators maintain more grey matter in brain regions linked to memory, emotional regulation, and decision-making *(Lazar et al., NeuroReport, 2005)*. This not only helps preserve cognitive function as we age, but also fosters resilience, calm, and mental clarity.

Meditation works best if done daily! Whether you choose guided meditation, mindfulness, or simply sitting in silence and focusing on your breath, meditation is a practice that nourishes both body and mind.

For something that costs you nothing, and you don't have to do anything, it is an incredibly powerful tool to add to your day! Meditation helps you reconnect, so your intuition becomes your guide again.

Next Tool - Journaling – The Window to Your Mind

If meditation is a window to your soul, journaling is a window to your mind.

The act of writing down your thoughts, emotions, or insights is one of the most powerful ways to process stress and uncertainty. When we're in a stress response our brain floods our body with cortisol and shifts blood flow away from the logical frontal lobe to the extremities so we can fight, flee, or freeze.

When you combine journaling with EFT and meditation, you begin to shift those stress-filled emotions out of your system and on to paper, where they can no longer control you.

I've been journaling on and off for more than 30 years. The entries I wrote during the early years, prior to our son's autism diagnosis, became my first book, *David's Gift*. Many readers said it felt like I had lived in their home, the entries were raw and totally honest. Journalling helped me make sense of the challenges we were going through and inadvertently helped so many others. What I came to realise, is that despite our circumstances, we are more alike than we are different, especially during our peri-menopause years.

So many readers told me they could totally relate to the emotional rollercoaster they were living with because the stress, the tears, the thoughts and the feeling of being out of control, were the same. One day, feeling strong and confident clear. The next day, feeling lost and overwhelmed.

Reading those journals now, I wish I had used them more intentionally to advocate for myself with my doctor, to identify patterns and to heal more consciously. But even unintentionally, those journal entries helped me process the emotion and provide clarity. And they still do.

Every year, I reread my journals and am amazed at my own growth. So often we don't recognise how far we've come until we see it written down.

Journaling reveals patterns, especially those automatic 'go-to' responses we repeat without thinking. It's a powerful tool for awareness. And with awareness comes the ability to choose differently. It also helps with identifying cycles of physical symptoms, so that you can share that with your medical practitioner, with clarity.

I often journal in the morning about how I felt the day before, any emotional triggers, or meditation insights. I also write out my big dream promises to myself and choose one small action to move closer to that dream each day.

There are no rules. Some days I write a page or two. Some days it's just a sentence. Some months I write every day, other times just once a week. The key is to start.

If you're not sure what to write about, try these prompts:

- What challenged me yesterday?
- What made me feel joy?
- What triggered me emotionally?
- What pattern am I noticing?
- What am I hoping for today?
- How are my energy and stress levels today?

And if you ever wonder whether your thoughts are worth writing down, just remember we have somewhere between 12,000 and 60,000 thoughts a day. Research suggests 80 per cent of them are negative and 95 per cent of them are the same as yesterday.

That's why journaling works. It interrupts the cycle, allowing you to see patterns you didn't know existed.

Tool #4 Gratitude – The Window to Your Heart

Practising gratitude every day is one of the quickest and most reliable ways to move from stress to joy.

In his book *The Happiness Advantage*, Harvard researcher Shawn Achor shares that when people spend just two minutes a day journaling three things they're grateful for (for 21 days), their brains begin to scan for positives, and their happiness increases dramatically.

The secret is to find **three new things** to be grateful for every day.

When I first began a gratitude practice, I repeated the same things every day: the sunrise, my family, the safety of my kids. But once I committed to finding three new things each day, something shifted. I became more present. I went out of my way to create opportunities for gratitude and kindness.

One day at the grocery store, the young cashier asked if I wanted my seafood bagged separately. I smiled and said, *"Thank you for asking, yes please, and thank you for being so good at your job."* His face lit up. That simple moment of kindness in acknowledging that young man made me feel good all day. He on the other hand may have thought I was a weird old lady, but that smile on his face said it all.

That's when I realised: gratitude is not just a thought, it's a feeling, that lives in your body.

Since then, I look for daily opportunities to practise kindness and feel grateful every day; a thank-you email, a wave at a courteous driver, a compliment to a stranger. These small acts change your state, and collectively, they can change the world.

Whether your gratitude practice is written, spoken, or shared, make it a daily habit.

But none of these tools will work unless you do them.

I often hear people say, *"I can't meditate."* My response? Try two minutes. Or go for a walk without your phone. Just be present. As for journaling, just start. There are no rules. And EFT? Try one round and notice the shift.

You can do all four practices: EFT, meditation, journaling, and gratitude in under 30 minutes a day. And the benefits will transform not only your leadership, but your life.

These are the tools that will help you rise as a **strong, clear, and unapologetic** feminine leader.

CLEAR

Principle # 6 Honour Your Personality

There's no such thing as a 'one-size-fits-all' approach to anything. Just because you saw someone on Instagram lose 50lbs from a new diet or exercise program doesn't mean it will work for you. And you might not be able to authentically replicate that style of leadership you learned from a man at his very expensive three-day leadership seminar.

For years I have been coaching women through wellness, fitness and leadership and what I know to be absolutely true - is that we are divinely unique. We all have different personality types which require us to learn how to embrace and adapt knowledge so that it honours that uniqueness.

The trick is first understanding you.

Through my counselling studies I developed a profile test which has evolved through my years of coaching work, to become the Mid-life Reimagined Personality Profile. It divides us into four personality types with certain needs that if not met, can make you feel low in energy, triggered easily or cause you to judge yourself unfairly.

These personality types show you how to 'fill-up' your emotional and physical energy banks.

To discover your unique personality type is head to my website **Mid-Life Reimagined:** https://mid-lifereimagined.com and click on Quiz.

There are 4 Personality Need Types....

Strong need for Self Recognition **ACHIEVER**	Strong need for Social Involvement **SOCIALIZER**
Strong need for Self-Fulfillment **COMPETITOR**	Strong need for Security **PEACEMAKER**

Achiever - Strong need for Self-Recognition

Usually successful at what you do. Once you make your mind up to do something you have the ability to draw on an incredible amount of inner energy and determination to complete a task.

Achieving perfection is especially important to you; hence you may miss out on some challenges, preferring to master a task before putting your hand up to attempt opportunities that come your way.

While self-recognition is important to you, you also like to be noticed and acknowledged for your success. And if you do not receive that outside acknowledgement, it can create doubt or frustration.

You tend to take criticism hard and personally, which can affect your self-esteem and confidence. Why? Because you are naturally self-critical and do a fine job of being self-judgemental. Hearing it from others just makes you feel worse!

Because you are achievement oriented, you often find it hard to celebrate your success in any project. Instead, your natural, self-critical self may tend to focus on any perceived failings – such as finding the missing comma on page 56, paragraph five, line 10 of the 200-page document you took months to prepare!

Important Things to Remember

Although you like being with a group you probably achieve better results on your own. You like to socialise but are more likely to prefer thought provoking conversations over general chit-chat.

It is important to recognise and understand your high and low energy times and adjust your work schedule accordingly.

Probably your greatest downfall is self-criticism and self-judgement. You take a long time to bounce back from perceived failure.

You are a natural born leader; however, your high standards and strong work ethic often make it difficult for you to delegate effectively as you often prefer to do things yourself. Your personality type needs to be mindful of being critical and allow others to step up into their own brilliance, mistakes included.

Best Wellness Practises for You

While you are often self-motivated, you have a need to feel as if you are achieving, and like others to notice those achievements, otherwise you quickly lose motivation.

Small, incremental (even daily or weekly) intentions work best for you. And releasing the need for approval or acknowledgement from others will go a long way to help you trust your intuition rather than the drive to be noticed or acknowledged.

EFT is a perfect modality to help reframe your naturally critical self-talk that shows up as procrastination, self-imposed limitations and the Imposter Syndrome!

While you do not mind exercising, best practices for you are often either working out with a group of people who are also achievement focused or creating a workout regime for you where you can see results. Exercises such as push-ups or strength challenges, taking part in classes where you can master a particular skill or challenging yourself to increase your walking or running times, rather than being a certain weight or body size, will keep your motivation high.

Listening to motivational or self-improvement audio books and podcasts, while you are working out, is the ideal practice for you. You are often the multi-tasking queen—improving your mind while you are improving your body just makes perfect sense to you!

While you probably know a great deal already about diet or wellness programs, you tend to become a bit evangelical or obsessed with certain programs. Remember for you, incremental steps are important.

Socializer – Strong Need for Social Involvement

You are a people person. Not always in the limelight, although you don't mind being noticed every now and then, you are more likely to be the one invited to a party for your great people/conversational skills, rather than the one dancing on the table with the lampshade on your head!

You are generally easy-going, although in your endeavour to have fun in your life, you often do not say what is really on your mind and would rather avoid conflict than confront it. You are often a great diffuser of uncomfortable situations and will seek to find humour or a way to negotiate the best possible solutions for everybody.

But this can sometimes create challenges for you emotionally, as you can overlook other people's agendas. You tend to take everybody at face value, because having a large group of diverse friends is an important part of your personality needs profile.

However, because of that, you may ignore your intuition in some circumstances and make friends with people you think have your best interests at heart, only to find later they were not as they appeared to be. When people hurt you, you are often shocked, while others will say *"I told you so!"*. That is why learning to listen to, and trust, your intuition is key for keeping your emotional needs balanced.

Important Things to Remember

You are a likeable leader. You have an innate ability to make people feel good about who they are. You find your energy being with people, so you have a high need for connection and generally dislike doing things on your own. Workplaces with high people contact, networking, memberships to organisations, or involvement in charity work helps you maintain your energy.

Your downfall could be sticking to your wellness intentions during periods of high social events—think Christmas, Easter... or any other reason for that matter!

You love an excuse for a get together with friends and often enjoy planning social gatherings. However, you often burn the candle at both ends as you're probably the last to leave a party if the music is still playing. In turn, sticking to your work-out and eat well plan, can be forgotten!

Best Wellness Practises for You

Working out or exercising on your own is the worst thing for you, and you will find your motivation drops very quickly if you are doing something that is routine or boring.

The best form of exercise for you is something that involves people, and the idea of making friends and socializing at the end of whatever you do, can be enough to keep your energy levels high.

Group gym or yoga classes, running clubs, walking with a friend and group sports are the best types of workouts for you.

EFT and meditation are perfect practises for you to release the past hurts of people who have let you down and the shame of not seeing it! These will help you identify and clear those past patterns.

While you like to practice healthy eating, your downfall is food and alcohol when socializing. Networking breakfasts, coffee catchups or drinks after work are your idea of essential practises. So intermittent fasting, getting adequate protein and fibre and making sure you are drinking plenty of water throughout the day are two things that can work for you to keep your energy levels balanced.

Peacemaker - Strong Need for Security

You are reliable, loyal and dependable. You can be introverted; dislike being put on the spot and tend to shy away from anything that involves being in front of the group. But you are the person everyone relies upon in the storm.

A great listener, people often gravitate to you naturally to tell you all their problems. You would make a great counsellor; you may not always know what to say, but you know how to listen.

As a leader you often put other's needs before your own, and you may find confrontation very difficult. Because of that, you tend to take on more than you should, causing both your physical and emotional energy levels to fall very quickly.

You need to create strong emotional and physical health boundaries as a priority as that old 'reliability' gene may stop you from being able to say NO when you need to!

While you naturally have strong intuition, you can often overlook that in your desire to not rock the boat. You tend to keep your emotions close to your chest because speaking your truth can be an uncomfortable experience for you. You are naturally intuitive and compassionate, but you can be seen as a pushover. It is much safer to keep your opinions to yourself while eating a bowl of chips, or a block of chocolate, than to overcome the fear of confrontation.

Important Things to Remember

You persevere through difficult times so once you have set an intention you usually don't mind the hard work behind it.

You often need time to think to make sense of situations, but do not let that dissuade you from speaking up. Other personality types often speak before they think—you are the opposite. You need time to process your thoughts and when you speak it is usually very wise and profound. But because you are slow to speak up, others may think you have nothing to say. However, it is exactly the opposite. You usually have a lot to say; you just need to feel confident and be given the time to say it.

Learn to trust your intuition and speak your truth, even if your voice shakes.

Best Wellness Practises for You

Thoughtful activities are best for you to protect your energy. Yoga, Pilates, Barre classes, walks either on your own or with others are where you often find your motivation.

If you work in an environment where there are lots of people, you need to ensure that you are taking regular re-charge breaks to fill up your emotional energy banks.

Peace and harmony in your life are essential to finding your 'Zen'. Reading, creative activities, taking time out for solace and spending time in beautiful, peaceful places are all important in keeping your energy levels high.

While meditation is not difficult for you, setting aside time to practise it may be, as you often put everybody else's needs first. Make it a priority in your day.

EFT/Tapping is a brilliant practice for you to do daily to build your confidence and belief in yourself. You may be carrying a lot of hurt from past experiences because you feel so deeply. Releasing the emotional connection to those memories will go a long way to helping you release that weight that no longer serves you, first emotionally and then physically.

You are the hardest person on yourself. Practice and celebrate your ability to be still and quiet. The world needs more people like you.

Competitor - Strong need for Self-Fulfillment

You are usually strong, positive, and dominant. Leadership comes naturally to you as you have high energy levels, but you may find working with others rather frustrating. In fact, people skills are not normally your forté, and you may find yourself in trouble as you tend to 'step on other people's toes' in your attempts to achieve your, often, impatient success.

You have great entrepreneurial skills as ideas come to you at all times of the day and night. Sticking to the original idea can sometimes be a problem for you, and allowing others to catch up may be frustrating.

One of your challenges to overcome may be your ability to want to control your life (and those around you). Try and get into the habit of listening to others and hearing their point of view.

Goal setting is usually not an issue for you as you are often a high achiever. You usually like to do things that match your high energy levels and competitiveness. You need to surround yourself with those who can adapt to your high energy and drive. You are naturally suited to leadership rather than managerial roles!

Important things to remember

Patience and trusting others can be your biggest downfall. As a naturally high-energy and self-motivated person, understanding other's perceived weaknesses, in your eyes, can cause you to overlook other people's emotional needs. While you do not mean to do that, you are a person who has learned to just get on with things, and wallowing in perceived 'self-pity' is something you just don't see the need to do.

Hence, you may be carrying many deep wounds of the past that you chose to just build a bridge and get over. Vulnerability or intimacy may be very difficult for you, as in the past you may have been hurt because of it. So, you see the armour around your heart as strength. But this can stop you from creating strong, unconditional relationships as others may feel you do not hear them or understand them.

You may see solving problems or fixing broken things as your way of showing love because that feels solid to you.

Trusting your intuition is sometimes the last thing you will do, as you need data and facts. Showing your true self takes time, but when you do you are a fiercely loyal, powerful and protective being who makes others feel safe in a world that often feels unsafe.

Best Wellness Practises for You

Stress may be a problem in your life so exercise often takes on a different meaning for you as it can be an enormously powerful antidote for releasing stress that may build in your body. Areas to watch are your neck and shoulders where tension may build.

Competitive sports or exercising where you are pushing your own personal boundaries, such as marathons or weight training really suit your high energy personality.

Meditation is a very important tool for you, but one you may find challenging—as sitting still may seem like a waste of time for you! But finding 20 minutes every day to meditate will make a huge difference to your life.

EFT/Tapping is a powerful tool for you especially in releasing the hurts from the past where others may have taken advantage of the few times in your life you have allowed vulnerability. You hurt deeply and releasing that hurt will help you use your incredible confidence and power for good!

As far as food goes, you have a real tendency to be at either ends of the spectrum. Either super health conscious to the point of being extreme, or exactly the opposite, where others might worry about your excessiveness. Balance is key for you.

How to work with your energy types

The main thing to remember with this personality type is that it is not about behaviour, but more about how to keep your motivation and energy levels high, and your stress levels low.

Your personality type often moves from right to left and back again, but seldom from top to bottom. However, you may find that you have various aspects of each personality type, needing combinations from each to keep your energy levels high.

I identify as an Achiever, but there have been times in my life when I have had a strong desire for social interaction and connection, which was especially pertinent during the pandemic. That lost connection with others was not only felt deeply by me, but probably 90 per cent of the world's population.

Knowing that, I was also conscious of connecting virtually over Zoom or phone with my sisters and friends. While it is not necessarily fulfilling the physical connection, those small steps, implemented daily, helped me keep my social needs high and subsequently my energy levels high.

However, when I was working at a school, where social connection was very high all day, it was the opposite. I knew I needed to fulfill the Achiever aspect of my personality more to keep my motivation and energy levels high. So, during that time, instead of going to group gym classes, I worked out on my own while listening to podcasts or non-fiction books, as my need for self-recognition and achievement was high at that time.

A Peacemaker and a Competitor-type exist on a similar quadrant. Not needing that social interaction as much, it can drain you.

Most of the Peacemakers I have worked with need to guard their energy levels fiercely as they can get overwhelmed and exhausted very quickly, especially when demands on their time and energy overstep their boundaries. While Competitors are often more direct in creating their boundaries, sometimes they too can forget that people drain their energy rather than enhance it. So, self-care, time out and time alone are high priorities.

The Personality Profile is a guide to help you identify your self-care needs. Once you understand the importance of setting up those habits, you can go a long way to ensuring that your energy and motivation levels stay high.

Clear

Principle #7 Live Purposefully

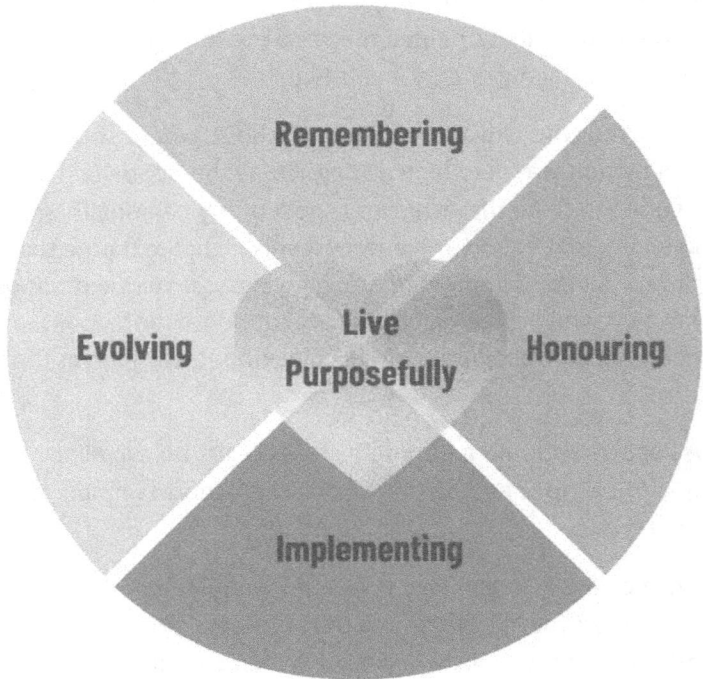

Being able to lead in a strong, clear, and unapologetic way begins with connection—connection of your mind, heart, and body. When the 'who' you are, the 'what' you do, and the 'how' you do it all align, because you are living purposefully.

We all come into this world with a purpose. We know it when we're born. In fact, most of us still carry that knowing until the start of school. But then people, words, and events of childhood interrupt that knowing. We learn how to adapt. To sit still. To behave. To be accepted. To follow rules. And in many cases, we stop doing what we love because we're told there's no future in it. Along the way, that inner knowing is lost.

Some are fortunate. They grow up with parents and mentors who see their purpose and support them to live it. But for many of us, it becomes elusive.

Usually because we're looking in the wrong place.

One of the most powerful, life-changing and liberating experiences I've ever had was the moment I discovered my Soul purpose. Perhaps even more profoundly, I saw why I had it so wrong in the past.

I didn't know how to have a purpose when I was younger. I'd hear people talk about it, but thought some people had purpose and others just didn't. I loved writing stories but wasn't great at grammar, according to my fourth-grade teacher, so I took that as not being good at writing. I loved making up plays and dances to perform for my family, but after forgetting the words while singing in front of the whole school at age 10, I believed I wasn't good at that either. I loved teaching and playing 'school' with my siblings, but my Year 11 Careers Counsellor told me I wasn't smart enough to be a teacher. I loved mentoring and inspiring others, but other than captaining sports teams, I had no idea how to turn that into a career.

So, I became a secretary.

I wasn't particularly good at it, but at least it paid the bills. My 20-year-old self was a young woman adrift, searching for something she didn't know existed. I started believing there wasn't anything more to life and maybe I'd been wrong for even hoping there was. No wonder I sought comfort in food; it numbed the emptiness. Exercise became my outlet, the way I tried to release all the sadness and frustration I didn't know how to express.

I was bored and uninspired. Before a ski trip with friends I remember thinking, *"Maybe skiing will be my passion."* Then I fell off the ski lift and had to walk down the slope carrying my skis. So much for that.

A few years ago, I was still wrestling with the idea of Soul purpose. Why do some people have one and others don't? I started journaling with the Four A's framework I spoke about in Chapter 5:

- I now allow myself to live with purpose.

- What do I love to do, and know I'm good at?

- I choose to step into my purpose, without judgment.

- How does it feel when I'm doing what I love?

Not long after, I attended a networking lunch and sat next to a woman, in what can only be explained as true serendipitous moment. We started talking about purpose and during our conversation, she shared a Carl Jung quote that struck me deeply:

"What you did as a child that made the hours feel like minutes - herein lies the key to your earthly pursuits."

Something about it felt like the answer I'd been waiting for. I grabbed a business card and scribbled the quote on the back so I wouldn't forget it.

At first, I didn't see how it applied to me. But the next day, while working out, I thought of my kids, and it suddenly clicked.

My son David used to walk around our backyard with a big stick, narrating imaginary adventures. He could master any computer game by age two. He's now a talented video editor, telling impactful and entertaining stories, through film.

My middle daughter was always full of stories. From the moment she got in the car after school, she'd launch into detailed tales about her day. She's now a multi-award-winning TV news journalist.

My youngest danced constantly and had incredible tenacity, focus and determination to master any new skill. She was also the most persuasive 4-year-old I had ever met, She began a career in dance, but quickly moved into management, and now a successful career in sales—using her stage presence, people skills, and persuasive sales skills to excel in her career.

And me? At four, I loved telling stories, teaching, and performing. My siblings thought I was bossy. I now know I was just living my Soul purpose!

The next step was channelling my epiphany into something I could do now. Years ago, a business coach was helping me define my brand by using the word 'Help' but it never really resonated for me. 'Help' leaned into therapy or counselling, and while I am also a trained counsellor, it is not the thing that really lights me up.

Then one day it hit me—what I truly love is to **teach**. I love facilitating seminars. I love speaking from stage, taking complicated ideas and breaking them down into powerful learnings, and I love coaching and mentoring. I love finding the humour in life and sharing insights through social media videos.

I used to have weekly life-coaching segments on a radio station in Australia and the host once said, *"You have a way of being both inspiring and entertaining.*" I never plan it. It just happens EASILY. That's Soul purpose, the thing you do that comes easily to you, that others see as hard.

Once I embraced those three words - teaching, inspiring, entertaining - everything aligned.

"Help" drained me. "Teach" energized me.

Now I see the same thing in so many women I coach. The stories may be different, but the patterns, the self-doubt, the self-sabotage are the same.

- Women who wanted to live their purpose but were ridiculed for it.

- Women who knew their passion but were never given the opportunity to pursue it.

- Women who gave up doing what they loved to raise a family.

- Women who never knew what their purpose was and believed that was just how life worked.

That disconnection from our Soul purpose creates a deep ache in the heart. Whether we don't know what our purpose is, or fear living it, or anything in between—it hurts.

But when you reconnect with your Soul purpose, you shift into a lightness of being. Bringing joy and confidence and a feeling of belonging. It helps you make sense of your life and the journey that's brought you here.

When we don't live our purpose it's painful. So, we numb the pain with food, compulsive exercise, unhealthy relationships, alcohol, gambling, or any other addiction that helps us avoid the ache.

What I've found, for most people, is that the greatest source of joy comes from discovering their unique Soul purpose. Their reason for being here.

So many times, I've asked a client what they want, and they respond with, *"I don't know."* I'll ask what they think their Soul purpose is, and again the response is often, *"I have absolutely no idea."* And that breaks my heart.

To live 80 or 90 years on this planet and never experience the joy of fulfilling the reason you came here. That's heartbreaking.

Soul purpose is who you are. Life purpose is what you do.

Soul purpose never changes. Life purpose evolves as you do.

We often get so hung up on *life purpose* that we miss the deeper truth: we have two. Soul purpose remains constant. Life purpose is how you express it at any stage of life.

Your purpose doesn't have to be earth-shattering or world changing. It's simply living with intention. Taking that spark, that talent, knowledge, or insight that's unique to you and expressing it.

All the things I loved as a child, those were my soul's whisperings. I just didn't know how to listen.

So now it's your turn.

Take a moment and recall what you loved at age four. Can't remember? Ask someone who knew you then. Or imagine it now.

Then, choose 1–3 words to describe your Soul purpose. From there, explore how your life purpose can evolve to express it.

When I taught aerobics, I was teaching, inspiring, and entertaining. It lit me up. I could teach four classes a day, choreograph four more in between, and it felt effortless.

When I worked in marketing I loved working creatively on new marketing projects, interacting with parents and mentoring students, but I dreaded the stats and spreadsheets.

In my current work, I get to tell stories, inspire change, and keep it engaging. That's my sweet spot.

Here are some Soul purpose clues to consider finding your sweet spot:

•Loved listening and supporting others? Consider a career in counselling, coaching or mentoring – formally or informally.

•Were you called bossy, or naturally initiated new friendship groups wherever you went? You are probably a natural born leader.

•Loved building or making? Consider a career in architecture or design. Or perhaps working with startups or student incubators.

•Always organizing? Consider a career in planning events or managing teams.

•Loved numbers? Use your skills to guide, teach, or manage money.

Your Soul purpose is meant to be lived through. Give yourself space to rediscover it and let it guide your life purpose. Because when the two align, your heart, mind, and body do too, and life begins to flow effortlessly with joy, ease, and deep fulfilment.

But Why Are We So Scared of It?

Years ago, I was watching Oprah Winfrey interview Dr. John Gray, the author of *Men Are from Mars, Women Are from Venus*. At the time, the book was a runaway bestseller, and for both men and women, a breakthrough insight into how each gender views love and relationships.

Oprah asked Dr. Gray, *"Why did it take you so long to publish this book?"* He replied, *"I knew this was my life's work. I had written books before, without fear. But this one? This one was important. And if I failed at it, I don't think I would've ever recovered."*

In all my years of doing this work, I've found that the fear of failing at something you're truly passionate about is the single biggest reason we never start. Or we start but create all kinds of reasons or excuses to stop.

Because failing privately is much less painful than failing publicly.

When I first began my professional speaking career, I was invited to speak at an event—sort of the warm-up speaker before the headliner. The main speaker, a well-known Australian women's doctor, was talking about how hormones affect weight. I was asked to speak about intuitive eating and the importance of strength training for menopausal women.

At the time, no one had even heard the term *intuitive eating*, so I felt nervous and exposed, especially when every health and diet expert around me was still preaching low-fat everything. Other than teaching fitness classes and calling out "5, 6, 7, 8!" over loud music, I had never spoken to a large group for an extended period.

About two months before the event, the organiser told me they were hoping to attract 500 women. That gave me plenty of time to prepare.

But instead, I procrastinated. Big time.

Every time I sat down to work on the presentation, I'd find an excuse not to. And not just any excuse — important ones! Like cleaning the fridge, hanging out the washing, or suddenly realising the windows *had* to be washed.

Two nights before the event the organiser called and said excitedly, *"Just checking in! We're sold out – 500 tickets sold!"*

She was thrilled. I was *terrified*. I wanted to say, *"Sorry, I must wash my hair that night!"* With less than 48 hours to go, all I had written was, *"Good evening, my name is…"*

Cue panic. Full-blown, heart-racing, deep-regret panic. It was way too late to back out; my name was on the poster. So, for the next two days, I fluctuated between terror and giving myself pep talks. At one point, I even wished for a severe case of laryngitis!

By 6pm the night of the event, I *sort of* had a 20-minute talk prepared but honestly, not really. I had no idea how I was going to pull it off.

As the organiser introduced me, I'm sure people in the front row could hear my heart thudding. There were 499 women in the room and one man. And of course, that one man was sitting dead centre in the front row, arms folded. He probably thought, *"What has my wife dragged me into?"*

But to me, he became the only person I could see. And in my head, I thought, *"This is awful. I'm awful. What am I doing here?"*

I rushed through my 20-minute presentation in about 17:30 minutes flat. As I finished, I thanked the audience and practically ran off stage.

Then the doctor took the microphone and with poise and confidence said, *"What a brilliant presentation on the importance of intuitive eating during menopause. It's a concept I hadn't considered before. I'm sure many of you have questions for Sally, I think that talk could've gone on for a bit longer. Sally, you'll be sticking around, won't you?"*

I wanted the ground to swallow me whole.

After her talk, we stood at the front of the room as people lined up to ask questions. I looked up, and the line of women wanting to speak with me stretched all the way to the back of the room. I was still there, answering questions, as they were packing up the chairs.

It took me a long time to understand what happened that night.
Why did I procrastinate so much?
Why did I fixate on that one guy in the audience?

Now I know.

That was the first time I ever shared what's now in this book.

I was passionate about intuitive eating. I was challenging everything the fitness industry was preaching. I was telling my truth. But deep down, I was terrified. Like Dr. Gray, I was scared of failing at the one thing I believed was my life's work. So, I found every reason not to do it (but my house had never been cleaner!).

I was trying to fail privately. Trying to avoid the pain of ridicule. What if they laughed at me?

What if I was wrong? What if that famous doctor criticised me publicly? I didn't have a degree. I had failed Year 12. I wasn't 'smart enough' to be a teacher. All those old voices came flooding back.

And worst of all, what if what I believed wasn't even true? What if everything I'd learned, healed, and overcome... was just *my* story, and didn't matter to anyone else? That's why this book has taken 25 years to write.

Even though I've written and published two books before *this* one felt different. It felt like my true work. And that was scary.

Because this time, it felt like stepping off a cliff with no safety harness. Like challenging the status quo. Like going up against people with degrees and scientific data and authority.

It felt... terrifying. What if I screwed it up? Who was I to think differently? I'm just a girl from the suburbs of Melbourne. I'm 69 years old. What gives me the right? Blah, blah, blah.

Here's what I've learned:

Soul purpose has no rules, and it doesn't require permission.

You don't need qualifications to follow your Soul purpose. When you're in flow, when you're open, questioning, aligned, *that* is what makes you qualified. In fact, Soul purpose often feels so effortless that we don't value it.

Whenever I'm facilitating a seminar, there's a moment when everything shifts. The air feels different. Time seems to pause. I never know exactly what I'll say, but the words come. And I know I'm in that space when I see it in people's eyes.

They're not just hearing my words—they're feeling something. Their heart space is opening. A light switches on. Suddenly, something that had been confusing or painful makes sense. I see it in others too —in Gerry when he's creating a piece of art. In my son, when he's editing a video. In one daughter, when she's sharing a story on camera or writing a new song. In the other, when she seemingly effortlessly closes a tough business deal.

There's a moment when everything just *clicks,* and what you do feels effortless. That's Soul purpose aligning with life purpose—whatever your life purpose looks like in that moment.

So why are we so afraid of it? Because we compare. We measure ourselves against other people's success, their looks, their Instagram-worthy lives. We think what we have to offer isn't valuable. We fear judgment. But here's the truth:

Your Soul purpose isn't something outside of you. It's *within* you.

Having a strong sense of purpose can also add years to your life. In fact, studies from both Japan's Blue Zones, and Western research, have found that people who live with clear purpose, whether through work, family, community, or creativity, are healthier, more resilient, and live longer.

As we are redefining our mid-life transition, this is especially important: purpose can reignite confidence, provide clarity and fuel the energy needed to lead and thrive.

Living strong, clear, and unapologetic is the journey back to yourself—when your mind, heart, body, and soul align. And when that happens, life becomes effortless and joyful.

Unapologetic

Principle #8 Speak Powerfully

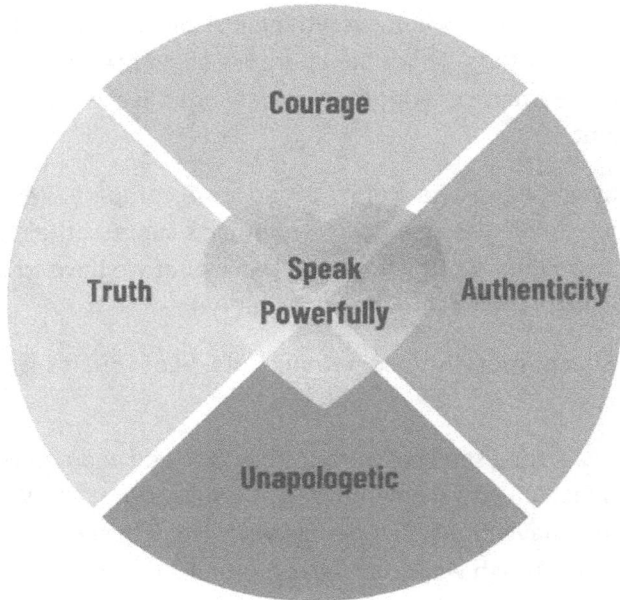

If there was ever a time to for women to step up and speak their truth, it is during our Menopause transition! For way too long, women have stayed silent about this most transformative time in our life. And because of that, we have created generations of women who have suffered in silence; been gaslit or ignored by the medical community; and worse, left their jobs, or held themselves back from applying for leadership positions, because they have been fearful of sharing the truth of what they are going through.

So why are women fearful about speaking about Menopause? Quite simply because they are fearful of being overlooked for promotion, judged as being old and past their best, or more insidiously, buying into their own fears about ageing. I was at a networking dinner one night, when two women sitting opposite me, asked what I did. When I told them that I facilitate menopause in the workplace workshops, both women shared that they were terrified of menopause. When I asked why one of them said, *"I'm scared that I will be judged as being old and past my use by date!"*

The other issue mid-life women face has been called the *Menopenalisation* phenomenon, where midlife women are ignored or overlooked in applying for jobs, or promotions because of their age. I coached a client recently who told me that she had applied for a job where she went through four interviews, and each time she was asked the same question *"When did you graduate?"* Even though interviewers are not allowed to ask an applicant's age, they were trying to figure it out, by aligning her graduation year. Another friend, a woman in her late 60's and a brilliant sales trainer, applied for 20 jobs, each time not even getting to interview stage.

This is the cost of us staying silent. Where menopause has been kept secret, and women have not shared both the challenges and gifts that come with this stage in our lives

And it is having a massive impact on business and the economy. In the HER BC report released in Vancouver Canada in 2023, shared some disturbing facts.

Unmanaged Menopause issues

- Cost Canadian Business $3.5B annually
- 540,000 lost workdays
- $237 million in lost productivity
- $3.3 billion in lost income for women who reduce their work hours or leave the workforce entirely.

The only way to turn this around, is to find our own courage to speak up, without fear or hesitancy. Not just about menopause, but in the boardroom and leadership as well.

One of our most powerful leadership qualities is the ability to speak in absolute alignment with what we believe to be true. But for many women, our voices have been quieted by judgment for so long, and speaking authentically and unapologetically, can be terrifying.

Many of my clients are still carrying the weight of old messages like: *"Children should be seen and not heard"*, *"Speak only when spoken to"*, or in my case, *"Do not speak until you've put your hand up and been invited to".*

When I think about how many women around the world are silenced, veiled, or restricted, it breaks my heart. And yet, in our free world, so many women struggle to speak their truth.

As a counsellor and EFT coach I've heard some incredibly painful stories and so often, I have heard the words,

"You're the first person I've ever told this to". That level of trust is sacred. It takes enormous courage to share something so private, to speak words that have been buried for years.

This work involves helping people release the emotional charge tied to memory. The memory remains but when the emotion is gone, it no longer has power.

I use many techniques (EFT is just one of them) to help people process and release trauma. But I often wonder: is the true healing in the tapping, or is it simply in telling the story out loud, for the first time, and finally letting go of the secret? Emotional fear, doubt, and pain live in the body. When we acknowledge it, feel it, and release it, we feel lighter.

One of my clients—let's call her Jane—had been emotionally and physically abused as a child. She was raised by an extremely dominant but successful father and a loving, passive mother. Jane worked hard to achieve success, earning her MBA and eventually becoming a sales and marketing manager, leading a team of 10 in a company owned by eight men.

When she first came to me, she was deep in perimenopause. Along with brain fog, exhaustion, and anxiety, she felt constantly triggered. She wasn't sleeping well, and she often doubted herself.

Though she was capable and experienced, Jane found herself reacting in ways that shocked even her. *"I don't feel like myself,"* she would say. *"I'm good at what I do, but I can't seem to hold my ground, especially when dealing with my bosses."*

We worked together for six months. On one group call, Jane arrived visibly anxious and upset. Earlier that day, she'd had a heated confrontation with a team member. Though she knew her team member was right, she couldn't bring herself to advocate for her with senior leadership.

Everyone on the call could feel her distress. I asked if she'd be willing for me to ask her a question in front of the group and she agreed. I asked, *"Can you remember a time when you knew you were right, but felt completely powerless to speak up to someone in authority?"*

She paused, and after about 30 seconds she told a story. She was a child, when she overheard her father yelling at her younger sister, punishing her for something she didn't do. Jane had summoned the courage to stand up for her sister and tell her father he wasn't being fair. But the moment of bravery was met with fury. Her father screamed at her, then grounded her for a week.

What stayed with her wasn't just the punishment, it was the look in her sister's eyes. A look that said, *"You tried to protect me, and now you're being punished for it."* That moment cemented the idea that it wasn't safe to speak up.

As Jane told the story, we processed it together. Then, suddenly she laughed. Surprised, we all paused.

She said, *"Isn't it ridiculous? I let that story stay trapped in my mind for over 30 years! My father always seemed so tall and terrifying... but he was only 5'7"! And now he's old and frail. Yet I let that booming voice keep me silent for decades. I'm done. I'm done letting that story have power over me."*

Her entire face transformed before our eyes. She looked different—lighter, freer, younger. It was profound to witness. At our next group session, Jane told us she had apologised to her team member, then stood up to her boss and successfully negotiated a better compensation package for her whole team.

She's not the only client I've seen this happen to. In fact, I've seen it so often that when it *doesn't* happen, I know we haven't yet reached the root of the pain.

When you release the emotional charge from painful memories, it's like lifting the weight of the world off your shoulders. Your voice is no longer trapped. You're free to speak without fear or emotion hijacking your message.

But at the core of every situation where a woman struggles to speak confidently, two words lie beneath the surface: your value and worth.

The Secret to Speaking Powerfully – Courageously Honouring Your Value & Worth.

We can pretend we have everything under control, but those three mirrors never lie:

Our body. Our relationships. Our bank account.

Value and worth often show up in disguise—as procrastination, self-sabotage, or overwhelm. They influence how you nourish your body, how you allow others to treat you, and how you show up in every area of life. No affirmation, diet, or workout plan will change your life until you reclaim your own value and worth.

Self-worth is fragile. You can work on it for years and feel strong, until something knocks you down. A breakup. A failed business idea. A rejection. Menopause. And suddenly, it all feels like it's crumbling. The problem is we tie our worth to *what* we do, rather than *who* we are.

People don't treat you based on how *they* value you, they treat you based on how *you* value yourself.

When your self-worth is low your boundaries are shaky, your standards are negotiable, and you settle. Every thought, word, and action you take (or allow) reflects what you believe you're worthy of.

This took me a long time to understand.

I once worked for a woman who constantly made me question my value. I loved the job, but the hours were insane, and the pay was far below industry standard. Every time I asked for a raise she'd say, *"There's no money in the budget."*

So, I worked harder. I believed that if I could just prove myself, she'd finally see my value. I took on more projects, brought work home on weekends, and pushed myself to exhaustion. Then one day, after attending a breakfast networking event, I arrived at work an hour later than usual. She called me into her office and reprimanded me.

I was furious. I went outside, took off my shoes and stood barefoot in the grass, trying to ground myself. I called Gerry, who let me vent for half an hour. *"You know what she's like,"* he said. *"Why do you keep putting up with it?"*

I didn't have an answer.

I often think about that moment. I wish I'd said, "Back off, lady!" (Or any other word with four letters!)

But I didn't. I stayed silent.

Later, in an EFT session, I realised something powerful: She wasn't *attacking* me. She was *challenging* me. Challenging what I believed about myself. I stayed because I didn't value myself. She didn't need to devalue me; I was already doing it.

When I asked for a raise and she said no, I should've walked away. But I didn't. Because I had placed my worth in what I *did*, not in *who* I was. And when we give others the power to define our worth, we will always feel powerless.

That belief manifests in our bodies, our relationships, and our finances and shows up big time during the years of our menopause transition, because throughout that transition, everything about us—our body, our mind, our emotions and beliefs change. When you value your body, you don't abuse it. You don't starve it or feed it junk. When you value your mind, you don't speak harshly to yourself. You don't consume toxic media or waste time comparing yourself to others. We treat what we value with care.

Yet I know women who put more thought into what they put on their body rather than what they put in their body. This is why the phrase *"I choose to honour my body"* is so powerful. That one sentence gives you permission, maybe for the first time, to make choices that align with value and worth.

So how do you start building self-worth to speak courageously?

1. Stop hanging out with people who make you feel small.

Whether it's friends, co-workers, or Instagram accounts— if they make you feel 'not enough,' step back. Years ago, I made the decision to stop investing my energy into people who made me feel invisible. Now, I only spend time with people who leave me feeling *whole*.

2. Release the need to be a people-pleaser.

I spent the first half of my life trying to please everyone. When I stopped, everything changed. You cannot honour your worth, while constantly putting everyone else's needs ahead of your own.

3. Identify the places you are self-silencing.

When we self-silence to fit into a group, research has shown that it will impact on our physical and emotional wellbeing, especially in midlife. You did not experience all you have in your life not to share your wisdom. The key is to share your truth without the expectation of changing somebody's mind.

4. Do something just for you.

What is something you have been putting off for ages, that is just for you? A massage, a night with the girls, a weekend retreat? Just do it, without the need to explain it!

5. Don't justify your boundaries.

'No' is a complete sentence. If someone asks you to do something you don't want to, say no. No explanations. And when someone crosses a boundary, own your feelings. You don't have to convince them, just honour yourself.

5. Release all expectation of their response.

Your worth doesn't depend on how others react. You draw your line. How they respond is their business, not yours.

6. Be kind to yourself.

If I could tattoo one phrase on every woman's heart, it would be: **I AM ENOUGH.** You don't need to be a certain size, own a certain car, or have a certain job to be enough. Where you are right now is the result of your past choices and the stories you've believed in moments of vulnerability.

On this journey back to yourself, give yourself grace. Be patient. Be kind. You're learning a new way of being and unlearning decades of habits. It won't happen overnight.

But every small step you take, every moment you choose to honour yourself, builds your worth. Just try it... You may find that once *you* start valuing yourself, everyone else does too.

Identifying the Imposter Syndrome

If there is one thing that will certainly block you from having the courage to speak authentically, it's believing that haven't earned the right to be where you are!

I have a little secret to share with you. I've spent almost my entire life not having a single clue what I was doing. I've been reasonably successful in many areas, but for most of that time, I felt like I was winging it, just waiting for the day someone would find out. But usually, I could hide the doubt and carry on pretending like I had it all together.

Perimenopause changed everything, I just didn't have the emotional bandwidth to pull on the armour and pretend everything was OK.

Up to 75 per cent of people will experience Imposter Syndrome at some stage of their lives, and often we can create the coping strategies to overcome it easily. But when coupled with perimenopause and our fluctuating hormones, it can be the perfect storm.

The term *Imposter Phenomenon* was first identified in 1978 by Dr. Pauline Clance and Dr. Suzanne Imes. Since then, countless books have been written on the subject. One of those, *The Secret Thoughts of Successful Women* by Valerie Young, outlines five types of Imposter

Syndrome. When I read them, I was gobsmacked. I could relate to at least three. See if any sound like you:

The Perfectionist

You set impossibly high standards. You believe things must be perfect–your body, work, life– before you can be happy or successful.

The Superwoman (or Superman)

You take on more than anyone else and see rest as a weakness. You're probably reading this book while also mentally running through your to-do list, checking your phone, and feeling guilty for taking time out.

The Natural Genius

You seem to succeed effortlessly but behind the scenes, you work incredibly hard. You avoid things you're not immediately good at. You get praise, but think, "I could've done better."

The Soloist

You believe asking for help means failure. You don't hire a cleaner or delegate, because you think it means you're not coping. You think success only counts if you do it all yourself.

The Expert

You feel like you never know enough. You believe you need one more course, one more certification, one more book and *then* you'll be qualified enough to speak up or step forward.

When I first read those five types, I saw a part of me in each one. During perimenopause, there was so much stress in my life. How was I going to create the best possible outcomes for our son without excluding our two daughters? Was I doing enough? Were there things I was missing? You can imagine what my brain was like at 2am every morning! It became all too much. That perfectionist, superwoman, natural genius, soloist and expert weighing heavily on me. Something had to give.

But besides the impact of the hormonal perfect storm, imposter syndrome and success often go hand in hand.

Women like Dr. Maya Angelou, Arianna Huffington, Charlize Theron, and Viola Davis have all shared how the Imposter Syndrome has impacted on them throughout their careers. When I share this content in seminars and show the five types on a slide, without fail every single woman in the room can tick off at least three.

The **Superwoman** is especially common. That treadmill of doing everything for everyone, feeling like you're failing at all of it, then having two chocolate bars and an energy drink for lunch because you're too tired to do anything else.

Imposter syndrome wears many masks. It shows up as:

- Procrastination
- Overwhelm
- Stress
- Anger
- Tiredness

And most damaging of all, it's one of the key reasons midlife women sabotage their leadership potential.

Let's look at how each type might play out in real life:

• **Perfectionist**: "My CEO asked me a simple question, and I blanked. I must be losing it."

• **Superwoman**: "I'll eat healthy this week–oh wait, there're school events, Mum's birthday, a work deadline... I'll get up at 4am to make sugar-free brownies." (She then grabs two chocolate bars at the gas station because she didn't have time to eat).

• **Natural Genius**: "Thanks for the compliment, but I've just ordered two books and signed up for a course to get better."

• **Soloist**: "I should be able to figure this out myself. If I ask for help, they will think I can't cope."

• **Expert**: "I've been reading about macros. It's the new thing. You're not going to eat *that,* are you?" (Thought, not said!)

Imposter syndrome speaks to one thing: **our belief that we're not worthy of success.** What I didn't realise was how perimenopause can be the ultimate trigger for all things 'I'm not worthy.'

Our hormones and our bodies change so much during these years, and the gas lighting and misdiagnoses from the medical community doesn't help. It's a time when we suddenly feel less sharp, less energetic and less appealing.

The weight I gained made me feel old and frumpy. I looked so much older as my skin became drier, and my hair became thinner. My emotions were all over the place. I had stopped listening to my body because I didn't trust it. I had slipped back into stress eating or not eating. I wasn't journaling. I wasn't meditating. I was drowning in self-doubt.

The only way back was to **find me again.** To uncover the patterns and beliefs that had brought me to that point. It wasn't about changing jobs or going on a diet, it was about figuring out why I felt like an imposter in the first place. I was sabotaging myself because I didn't understand what my body was going through and what made it worse was thinking I was the *only one* who felt that way. Finding out that many women throughout menopause felt the same? Weirdly comforting. It was a tribe I didn't know I belonged to.

So, how do you overcome Imposter Syndrome?

1. Recognise it. Fear, doubt, procrastination, overwhelm are red flags.

2. Accept it. Acknowledge it. Share it. You are not the only woman going through this.

3. Uncover the pattern. Ask yourself: What early messages did I hear? *Who do you think you are? Don't get too big for your boots. Just remember where you came from.* Or a myriad of other words that were often said when we were most vulnerable. Maybe when you shared an idea, expressed a dream, or wanted something different from your family and in that moment, instead of validation, you got ridicule or rejection.

In your menopause transition, these old words resurrect, big time. Perhaps you were able to mask them in the past or ignore them because you built armour, physical and emotional, to protect yourself. Now you are going through the greatest hormonal change of your life and that armour has gone.

But you don't need it. You are becoming that woman you were always meant to be. You don't need to change a thing, except how you think about yourself. You are not broken. You are not behind. You are *not* an imposter.

Reclaiming yourself, finding the confidence to speak your truth, means identifying where imposter syndrome stole your confidence and choosing to listen to your intuition again. This is the true journey back to *you* and your mid-life years are the perfect time to do it. Everything about you is changing, the belief in what's possible may as well happen too!

Unapologetic

Principle #9 Lead Authentically

To be nobody but yourself in a world which is doing its best, night and day, to make you everybody but yourself – means to fight the hardest battle which any human being can fight – and never stop fighting. Staying real is one of the most courageous battles that we'll ever fight.
...............E.E.Cummings

For 18 months I hosted a Facebook Live Show called **Isn't It Time.** For each show I chose a topic, spent days researching it and then asked myself, *"Where am I living this or not living this in my life?"* There was one topic that really created a lot of response–what authenticity really means.

The word authenticity is not a noun but a verb; a journey not a destination, and it changes as we do, especially on this menopausal journey. Why? Because as we drop the people-pleasing role, what we *do* care about changes. We begin to care more deeply about things that matter to us, and less deeply about things that do not. That changes how we choose to speak, act and be authentically ourselves.

As our brain rewires during this time, one word I find runs synonymously with 'authenticity' is the word 'courage.' You simply cannot separate the two.

Authenticity is not a word to describe something or somebody. In fact, if somebody tells me they are an authentic person, I question their authenticity! It is visible in the words you use and the actions you take every day. To lead with courageous authenticity means finding the strength and courage to let go of fear–of rejection, of confrontation, of being vulnerable, of being wrong, of standing in your truth when it may not be well received by others.

And perhaps the most challenging fear of all–letting go of the need to make everybody else happy! It is insidious and manipulative, and many times it is so ingrained in us from when we were little, that we don't even know we are doing it.

How many times in your life have you decided to do something based on how it would make somebody else feel? Whether it was choosing a career to make your father proud, or a partner to make your mother happy, or worse, self-silencing when you know something is not right?

Stepping out from that habit of putting your needs last and other's needs first is no longer considered a virtue—it impacts on your health. In fact, studies show that women who consistently put the needs of others ahead of their own, are more likely to experience autoimmune conditions and chronic diseases. Because when you are not living your truth, your body senses it. It never lies. When you are not being authentic to your own self, it will show up as weight, illness, pain, or worse.

You simply cannot embark on this journey of living a strong, clear and unapologetic life, without also embracing courageous authenticity and letting go of the need to please others first. Courageous authenticity is a practice. A conscious choice of how we want to live.

Oprah Winfrey once said *"I had no idea that being your authentic self could make me as rich as I've become. If I had, I'd have done it a lot earlier."*

We were all born to be our most authentic selves. As a toddler, if we wanted to grab that bright, shiny object off the ground, we didn't wait for approval or to check to see if wanting that object labelled us as selfish or greedy or upset somebody. We just went after that object no matter how many times someone tried to tell us we couldn't have it.

But then came the words over time, and the patterns started:

- You can't always get what you want.
- Think of others before yourself.
- Don't be greedy.
- Just because you want it doesn't mean you can have it.
- And the doozie …. Who do you think you are?

As these words are said to us repeatedly, they get locked in our way of thinking. We learn that what we want is irrelevant and adjust what we want to please others.

What I have found to be true, is that the journey to the truest authenticity of us, is like peeling back the layers of an onion. Each time we want to elevate our leadership, or step into a role that is outside our comfort zone, negative beliefs, and issues we thought we had dealt with, arise again. I have often heard the words *"But I already dealt with that block before"* from clients.

That learned response to play small, or worse, tolerate bad behaviour by others, simply shows up again to test our belief in ourselves.

To be courageously authentic means embracing our wisdom, intuition and experience, and overcoming the fears that stand in the way at each stage of our lives.

Stepping into a more challenging role is often highlights any aspect of ourselves we haven't dealt with.

There are two fears I find are often the most common challenges, for women who want to lead authentically.

1. The Fear of Confrontation

For many people, the fear of confrontation is the reason they stay in bad relationships, dead end jobs or reach for a packet of potato chips, rather than say what they really want to say. They will go to any length to avoid confrontation. In a seminar I ran many years ago, one of the participants began to cry when we started talking about fear of confrontation.

Astrid wanted to apply for a new leadership position at her company, one that she felt very qualified for. For years she had been working for a large insurance company, at middle management level. She always talked herself out of applying for any internal promotions, telling herself she was happy, but watched others being promoted. She knew in her heart she was more qualified than most of them, she was just too scared to apply in case they said no, or laughed at her, and it was frustrating her.

Along with this role came a whole new level of accountability, and while she had been secretly hoping for the opportunity to apply, it also scared the hell out of her.

Prior to this new role, her whole life was filled with stories of just doing what she was told and never standing up to anybody

I asked if she had ever tried to stand up for herself in the past where it had a profound effect on her. She looked at me with tears in her eyes and proceeded to tell her story.

Her father was an Eastern European man who had a quick temper and a loud voice. Her mother was very quiet and did whatever her husband wanted. They had emigrated to Australia in the 1970's and her father worked exceptionally hard to create a new life in a new country. He was a big man with an equally big, gruff persona.

Her mother had never worked outside the home, nor had she ever mastered English. Her memory of her mother was a woman who was satisfied with being a homemaker and threw herself into caring for her husband and her two children.

There was always plenty of good food in their house, but Astrid hated the lunches her mother made with crusty, large slices of bread from the Italian bakery filled with things like salami and mortadella. The kids at school made fun of her smelly sandwiches and odd-looking cakes her mother made and put into her lunch box. She just wanted to be like the other kids.

One night, while they were having dinner, she summoned up the courage to ask her mother if she could please take a normal sandwich to school, she just didn't want to look like that 'wog' kid. As soon as she said the words, her father exploded in rage. He accused her of not honouring her heritage and that wanting to be like the other Australian girls meant she also probably wanted to wear short skirts and sleep with boys as well.

No matter how Astrid tried to explain herself her father just got angrier, and out of the corner of her eye, she saw her mother with her head bowed, trying in vain to hide the fact she was crying.

Her father then yelled at her again, telling her she was responsible for hurting her mother and she had no respect. The last thing Astrid wanted to do was to hurt her mother.

As she was telling the story, she said, *"I look back on that 14-year-old girl and can feel immediately how mortified I felt. I couldn't get my father to understand what I was trying to say, and in trying to say it, I hurt my mother. I felt so ashamed. I really do think that it was then and there I decided that confrontation was scary, and it is easier to just stay quiet."*

Overcoming the fear of confrontation is a skill that requires first releasing the emotional trigger to the memory, then practising small ways in which you can begin to build that courage, especially if you have grown up in a house where confrontation was simply not encouraged. Six weeks later, Astrid applied for an upper management job and was thrilled when she was appointed into the position. She said *"My legs were shaking in the interview, but I kept reminding myself I was perfectly qualified for the job, and I could deal with any confrontation courageously!"*

2. The Fear of Rejection.

Do you remember the first time you had your heart broken? I bet you know exactly when it was and where it happened.

For me, it was my 16th birthday party. I had been 'going out' with a guy who was captain of the rowing team at a private school in Melbourne. When I say *going out,* I mean Tim and I met each other at mass at 6pm on a Sunday, not sit together, but sit so we could see each other, then he would walk home with me, and we would sit on the grass outside the fence at the front of our house and talk. All while my brother and three sisters would whisper and giggle, sitting on the other side of the fence.

This went on for a few months before he asked me to come watch one of his rowing competitions on a Saturday afternoon. From then, in my mind, we were a couple!

A few weeks before my 16th birthday, I summoned up enough courage to ask him to come to my party. I bought a new dress—it was blue cheesecloth with a sash, puffy sleeves and embroidered with small mirrors and yellow flowers. I thought it was so beautiful, and I matched it with a pair of 4-inch-high yellow clogs. I was quite the catch, I thought. (I couldn't walk very well, but I sure looked good!)

The night of my party, he didn't arrive till almost 10pm. He apologised and said that they had a late competition and that's why he was late, I didn't think any more about it. A few days later, my girlfriend Paula called me. She said, *"I have something to tell you, are you sitting down?"* I sat down on the back step outside the kitchen door– that's how far the phone cord stretched–to get some privacy away from the big ears of my brother and sisters.

She proceeded to tell me that one of the other guys from the rowing team had told her that there was no training on the night of my birthday, that Tim had been at another party with another girl, who he told everybody was his new girlfriend! I was heartbroken, I mean really, desperately heartbroken, as you only can be when you are 16.

The pain of that rejection stayed with me for a long time. During one EFT session where I was working on my fear of sales, I connected the dots. Not only was I fearful of rejection, but I was also fearful of being rejected over the phone. No wonder it was hard for me to ask for a sale on a phone call. That fear was deeply embedded in the amygdala, the memory centre of my brain, created from that old story.

Something you are experiencing right now can be connected to an event that took place many years before. For me, that fear of rejection permeated through so many aspects of my life, until I figured out where it came from.

So **how** do you practice courageous authenticity daily?

1. Be very clear on **what you *want*,** not what **you *don't want.***

Again, this clarity thing. Courageous authenticity is a doing word. But if first starts with having clarity in knowing what you want. Learn to reframe the questions you ask yourself. So that you stay open to synchronicity. Called Frequency of Illusion, it is that phenomenon where your brain goes looking for opportunities to support you. Have you ever wanted a certain car? You are clear on the make and colour – and the next thing, you see that exact model and colour everywhere! When you align with your deepest desires, opportunities will present themselves everywhere. Your only role then, is to stay in your authentic power to make those opportunities a reality.

2. Release the judgement of yourself and others

Have you ever tried not judging others? It's incredibly difficult. Gerry and I once challenged ourselves for a whole month to not judge others and pick each other up when we did it. But they happened so quickly–everything from commenting on political leaders, to making comments on the way other people drove, we did it all the time!

As much as we judge others, we also judge ourselves. It leads us to get caught up in striving for perfectionism, questioning our actions or words, or worse, holding ourselves back from uncovering our own true authenticity. As you embark on this new journey of leading authentically, you will come across people who will judge you.

A client of mine once told me of an acronym she uses whenever she feels judged by others: IPOV – *Interesting Point of View*. Whenever she feels somebody is judging her, she simply says to herself *"That's an interesting point of view"* and moves on!

What other people think of you is none of your business and releasing judgement of yourself, or the need to judge others, is an incredibly freeing way to live.

The Strength to Overcome Self Sabotage

Let's talk for a moment about our bodies and self-sabotage because for so many of us, it's the place where we sabotage ourselves the most, often without even realising it.

Honestly, in most of the seminars I have run, even if the focus starts elsewhere, this issue of body confidence and sabotage lies just beneath the surface of many women's confidence struggles. Maybe it's because we're women. Maybe it's because it often starts with comparing ourselves to our teenage peers and then comes the magazines, movies, and media drilling home the idea that the perfect thin, model-like body equals happiness and success. And without a doubt, it raises its head during perimenopause!

I once worked with a client—let's call her Jessica. She was married with four children and had an idea for a niche business. She found a gap in the market and launched a business that became profitable very quickly. Within 18 months, she had a team of four and the business was turning over well into six figures. But she was struggling. Staff turnover was high. She was snapping at her kids. Her desire for intimacy with her husband had almost disappeared.

She'd seen me speak at a conference on menopause and self-sabotage and reached out for coaching. In our first session, she told me she'd gained over 50 pounds since starting the business. She'd always struggled with her weight as a teenager but had managed to keep it under control, even after four kids. She proudly showed me a photo of herself on the beach in a bikini with her children. *"Why was it so easy for me to eat well and exercise back then?"* she asked. *"Now, I look successful on the outside but inside, I feel like a fraud."*

As we spoke, we uncovered deep trust issues, particularly in her team. She admitted to micromanaging and she knew it was driving her staff crazy. I asked her who was the first person she felt she couldn't trust, and her eyes dropped to the floor.

"My parents," she whispered. *"Both of them."*

When she was 11 years old her parents went through an acrimonious divorce. She was the eldest of five and her dad moved out. Her mum, who had always worked, took on a more senior role bringing in much-needed money but also required her working longer hours. Jessica became the caregiver. She cooked dinner every night and looked after her siblings before and after school.

She'd always blamed her father for the divorce, until the day she discovered her mother had been having an affair with a co-worker. She was devastated. Every day, her mother gave her money to shop for dinner for the family. Jessica was so hurt and angry with her mother, she began secretly buying herself chocolate bars and eating them on the walk home, hiding the wrappers deep in the garbage bin before anyone could see.

In her 40s, the pattern remained. When a workday was particularly stressful, or she had a confrontation with an employee, she'd drive to the store, buy a large block of chocolate, eat it in the car and then go home like nothing had happened. The shame storm would follow. She'd beat herself up. She'd start another "clean eating" regime, stick to it for a few weeks and feel good until the next emotional trigger hit. And the cycle would start again.

Stuffing Down Emotions, We Can't Talk About

Dr. Brené Brown has done incredible work in the area of shame. In her book *The Gifts of Imperfection*, she writes: *"Shame derives its power from being unspeakable."*

Jessica's shame about what she was doing in private was overwhelming. On the outside, she was a successful mother, businesswoman, and wife. But on the inside, she was silently falling apart. She told me, *"I feel like I'm dying inside. I've never told anyone this."* Then she laughed, *"As if they can't see it!"*

So many of us carry that kind of shame, and most of it begins in childhood. Maybe it was being told we were stupid; being laughed at for asking a question; or being shamed for how we looked or spoke. And for some, it runs even deeper.

Research shows that many survivors of sexual abuse carry immense shame, often for decades. And that shame silences them. In 2006, activist Tarana Burke began the

#MeToo movement and in 2017, actress Alyssa Milano brought it into the mainstream with a single tweet. Within 24 hours, it had been shared over half a million times on Twitter and more than 12 million times on Facebook.

The floodgates opened, and the stories weren't just from Hollywood. People from every industry and institutions - churches, schools, finance, sports, politics - they finally began to speak up. But why did it take so long? Because of shame. Because of fear. Because of the risk of not being believed. And I get it, because it happened to me, too.

My Own Shame Story

When I was 22 years old, about a year before I started our fitness business, I landed what I thought was a dream job, working for a powerful, connected woman I admired. She was smart, sassy, and seemed to know everyone. I idolised her. One Friday afternoon she told me to grab my coat. We were going to a business lunch with a couple of investors she was negotiating a deal with. I was so excited. Nervous, but honoured, she had never asked me to join her regular Friday lunches before, I felt very grown up.

The lunch was held in the private dining room of an exclusive hotel. There were multiple courses. Plenty of wine. By 3pm I picked up my bag to leave but was told the meeting wasn't over. We were heading upstairs to sign contracts. My boss hissed at me, *"You're not leaving now. This is important."*

Upstairs in the suite, the wine continued to flow. At some point, I realised my boss and one of the male investors had disappeared. The remaining man began to inch closer to me on the sofa. I stood up to go the bathroom and as I walked past the kitchen, I saw my boss having sex with the other man... right there on the counter.

I panicked, locked myself in the bathroom and sobered up very fast. I realised why I'd been invited. I was there to entertain the second man. I found my way out, with a made-up mumbled excuse, grabbed my bag and left. On Monday, I went to work expecting some kind of apology. Instead, at the team meeting, she publicly berated me. Told me I'd ruined her deal. Accused me of being naive. *"You knew what you were getting into,"* she spat. *"Don't play dumb with me."*

And what hurt most? The other men in the room said nothing. For years, I blamed myself. Was I naive? Was I being immature? Did I read the situation wrong? Was it *my* fault? That experience shaped me in ways I didn't understand at the time. It impacted my confidence. It added fuel to my already growing obsession with weight and body image. We didn't talk about things like that back then. We stuffed them down, and in my case, I either ate them, or starved them away.

Now with tools like EFT, I've been able to process that trauma. But back then, I didn't have the language, or the courage, to speak it. Shame, like resentment, is hard to talk about. It wraps itself around your heart and silently weighs you down. And because it feels unspeakable, we cope the only way we know how: We sabotage ourselves and tell ourselves stories that aren't true, letting those stories run our lives. This mid-life time of your life is the time to let go of those shame stories, rewriting a whole new way of lightness and freedom.

Honouring Our Tribe

Belonging creates certainty. It helps us feel safe. But what happens when you no longer fit in? When your beliefs shift? When you outgrow your tribe? We are wired for connection but as we grow, that connection can start to feel strained. But when *you* change, when you start honouring your boundaries, releasing limiting beliefs, and stepping into unapologetic leadership, it can be unsettling for the people around you. Your growth challenges their status quo. Your truth becomes a mirror for others, and sometimes, people won't like what they see.

So, what happens when your tribe is no longer your tribe? It can feel like walking a tightrope across a canyon – gripping a thin pole for balance, taking one shaky step at a time. Even when you *want* to change, your subconscious will pull you back to comfort. That's your brain's job: to keep you safe. Growth requires risk and discomfort, and that's where self-sabotage creeps in. Not because you're weak or you lack willpower, but because you're trying to protect yourself from emotions that were never acknowledged or processed in the past.

The Way Forward

This strong, clear, unapologetic life you're creating is about unwinding years of old stories.
Unlearning. Releasing. Reclaiming.

Every decision you make from now on must be about **honouring yourself**. When it feels like things are spinning out of control, go back to the 4 A's:

- **Allow** – "I allow myself to feel this."

- **Ask** – "What is this discomfort really trying to teach me?"

- **Affirm** – "I choose to stay in the discomfort because I know it will pass."

- **Acknowledge** – "This is a pattern I've played out before, and I now choose differently."

The answers will come if you honour yourself enough to ask those empowering questions. The sabotage patterns will begin to reveal themselves and with awareness comes freedom.

Unapologetic

Principle #10: Embrace Change Joyfully

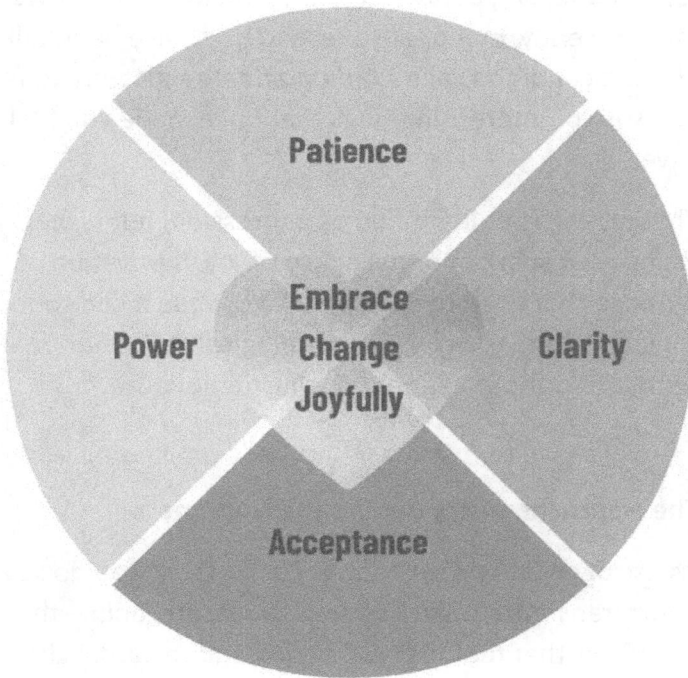

"Joy is not in things; it is in us.

Richard Wagner, Composer

When I made the decision to release old patterns as they arose and let go of preconceived notions of what living unapologetically really meant, I found I was constantly drawn to one word: 'Joy'. How do I find joy in this stage of my life, when some days it feels like a challenge just to face the day?

Many women talk about the menopause journey as being lonely and isolating. In fact, in the 2023 HER-BC survey released in Vancouver in 2023, 10 per cent of women reported feeling depressed during menopause. However, more recently, menopause researchers have been talking about a condition called **Anhedonia,** the inability to feel pleasure or interest in things that once made you feel alive.

That feeling isn't identified as depression, but rather, losing your spark and that sense of joy, motivation of purpose that used to drive you. And while it can sound clinical, for many of us, it is a biological and emotional recalibration that happens during menopause.

The Neurochemistry Behind the Numbness

As estrogen and progesterone fluctuate, so too do key neurotransmitters like dopamine and serotonin – the chemicals that fuel motivation, joy and reward. When estrogen drops, the brain's reward centre becomes less responsive. Suddenly what once felt exciting (work, connection, creativity) feels effortful or dull.

But this is not about mindset or laziness – it is a neurochemical shift. Then layer on midlife stress, ageing parents, raising teenagers, changing careers, global uncertainty – and cortisol takes the drivers' seat. Chronic, low-grade stress and anxiety suppress dopamine and serotonin further, leaving you emotionally flat. Our brain does this to protect you from overload... but also dampens your capacity for joy!

Reigniting Pleasure and Purpose

The wonderful truth about this, however, is that you can restore your spark and often it returns far brighter and more joyful than before. It's important to find ways to experience joy because it has been shown to improve both physical and mental health. It reduces stress, boosts the immune system, and improves cardiovascular health.

1. Move your body. I know I go on and on about this, but exercise boosts dopamine and endorphins naturally. Quite simply, you will never regret a workout, even though your brain can fight you on this. It can be challenging to get up early when it's cold and you haven't slept well but scheduling 30 minutes for a workout, whether it's in the gym or a walk, will make you feel so much better. Can't get out for a walk? Try getting off your chair and doing 10 power squats and just feel the energy life surge through your body!

2. Eat for your brain. I also include supplements such as Vitamin D – essential for helping to balance your mood, especially in countries where it's difficult to get daily sunlight; Good quality protein to help regulate blood sugar swings and fibre and fermented foods for good gut health; Omega-3 and B-vitamins and minerals can also help support mood regulation. Magnesium for deeper sleep and Creatine to help with brain health and muscle development. Reduce the amount of ultra-processed foods and stay away from foods that cause inflammation – especially industrial seed oils.

3. EFT/Tapping. This is one of the best and simplest ways to reduce stress and increase joy. It can feel like a weight being lifted off your shoulders, as decreasing stress helps you look at past stories through totally different eyes.

4. Other alternative therapies - Acupuncture certainly helped me, and I don't know what was in the little black pills the acupuncturist prescribed, but I certainly noticed a difference in less severity of the night sweats, and I was fortunate enough to not experience a hot flash.

5. Seek connection with people who make you laugh. Laughter and meaningful relationships raise oxytocin, your 'joy hormone'. When women are stressed, we resolve our stress best by 'tend and befriend'. Find the friend (or friends) who know and love you for who you are and are joyful to be around. I have two friends in particular who feel like soul sisters. We've laughed together, cried together, we speak the same language and have the same beliefs. We've had hours-long lunches and dinners and never run out of conversation. Before we leave our get-togethers, we have organised our next meet up and continue our conversations via Facebook Messenger, often a couple of times a day. Women thrive on good friendships!

6. Sleep deeply. Treat your sleep as importantly as you do your workouts! Sleep restores emotional resilience.

7. Revisit your purpose. When you do what matters to you, it reignites your brain's natural reward system, more powerfully than pleasure alone.

8. Find Joy in simple things. Take time to find joy in simple things. Sunrises or sunsets, flowers in the Spring and the colours of the trees in the Fall, the laughter of a child, hug a friend, tell someone you love them. Joy is simple to find, it exists everywhere, if you choose to find it.

Clarity brings Power

Our menopause and midlife journey is about accepting this time of change joyfully and patiently.

Menopause wakes us up. It is relentless in its ability to cause havoc when we don't listen. It is a change that continues to evolve – maybe for 10 to 14 years. If we don't adapt to those changes, if we don't listen to our intuition and trust in our body's wisdom it only makes the symptoms worse.

Most of all, it calls us to break the habit of disempowerment; the belief that it's somebody else's job to care for us, look after us, fix us, or take responsibility for us.

Disempowerment manifests itself in so many ways. Up until now, most women have readily handed over their power to the medical profession, often being gaslit, ignored, or worse, given medical interventions they didn't need or want. Because of the lack of investment into women's health research and funding *'they'* have been making assumptions about what is right for us and our body. So many women have told me that they have walked out of a doctor's office, after sharing what they are going through, only to feel worse than they did when they walked in.

That time ends now.

Menopause does not mean we are broken; it means that we are evolving from years of handing over our power, listening to advice from somebody who has not experienced this, and feeling disempowered to take our own health into our own hands.

While our menopause transition is the most intense hormonal event of our lives mainly because it lasts so long, when we embrace this change joyfully, seek knowledge, ask questions and become curious about this change in our body, everything changes. Intuitive ideas appear, coincidences occur, the right medical practitioner will appear at the right time.

Embracing Joy Within

So how do you start with this process? It starts by understanding...

> Our beliefs form our thoughts.
> Our thoughts create our emotions.
> Our emotions influence our words.
> Our words impact our actions.
> And our actions create our reality.

> If you don't like the last, it's simple, go back and change the first!

One of the most powerful ways to start that shift—right now—is to become mindful of the words you use. Your words are like a warning bell. They reveal what you truly believe, and they offer a path back through the ladder to uncover the deeper story underneath.

I'm always picking up on the language my clients (and my children!) use. At this point, it's like nails on a chalkboard when I hear disempowering phrases.

Words are *exceptionally* powerful. And so many of the phrases we use become such unconscious habits that we don't even realise we're saying them.

Hypnotherapist Marisa Peer says:

"Our minds cannot hold two conflicting thoughts—it will always default to the negative one."

Our subconscious mind responds to the words we use all the time—to describe ourselves, our lives, our bodies, our challenges. Those words *lock in* our reality. In other words: **your subconscious believes what you say.**

But how many times have you said or thought something... and then immediately contradicted yourself?

Like:

"I really want to get healthy, but I hate getting up early to exercise." Or:

"I'd would love a leadership role, but I don't want to work long hours." Or:

"I'm ready to find my soul mate, but I don't want to get hurt again."

Guess which part your brain remembers? The one that feels more emotionally charged—and most often, *it's the fear*.

So many of us say what we want, only to negate it seconds later. And that's exactly what we end up attracting into our lives.

But when you flip the script and make that second statement a joy filled *empowering truth,* your energy and focus shift too.

Instead of:

"I hate getting up early" try:

"I choose to get up early to move my body. I love the feeling of having more energy."

Instead of:

"I don't want to work long hours" try:

"I love having a career where I can lead with heart and soul."

Instead of:

"I don't want to get hurt again" try:

"I choose to attract a soul mate who honours my worth."

Or for what you are going through right now:

"I choose to embrace this change in my life with joy, patience and wisdom"

Notice how different you feel even *reading* those words? When you change the words you use, it shifts your emotions. It shifts your thoughts. And ultimately, it changes what you believe is possible.

Where you are right now—how your body feels, the relationships you're in, the career you're building—is the result of thousands of words you've spoken and tiny decisions you've made (or avoided) over years.

Joyful people speak with care. And it starts with your daily language.

If it feels hard to catch your own words, start by listening to others.

- Notice the words people use to describe their bodies, their jobs, their relationships.
- Notice the energy behind the stories they repeat.
- Notice how negative conversations reinforce the belief that *this is just how things are.*

Now more than ever, as you step into your own intuitive leadership, during this hormonal change, when your brain is recalibrating - your *words matter*.

When you use the 4 A's—**Allow, Ask, Affirm, Acknowledge**—you're not just speaking differently. You're aligning with your future self. You're rewriting the story.

So don't underestimate the power of the other words you use.

They are the subtle but mighty forces that shape your energy, your actions... and ultimately, your life.

Honouring You

In her book *The Menopause Brain* Dr. Lisa Mosconi, shares such valuable information about why our brain learns to function differently as estrogen levels shift. She explains that while this process can feel like living in a fog, on the other side of it, the brain is renewed.

Many women report that there comes a point in their lives when meaningless conversations became grating, and they can see right through those not being authentic.

For many of us, the pandemic was that turning point. It didn't make sense. The fear mongering was grating on the soul. The mind games were obvious and insidious. During this time, my tribe shifted. Nothing we were being told felt truthful. And yet, like-minded people—many of whom were being silenced and vilified for questioning the narrative—somehow found each other.

It became a catalyst for critical thinking and deep introspection. I think I must have said, *"This doesn't make sense,"* at least six times a day.

During this time, I created a Facebook group called *Influential Sovereign Woman*, and within a month it had grown organically to over 1,000 members—just through word of mouth.

Women who had been isolated or even vilified by their own families for trusting their intuition and questioning the narrative. Women who were uninvited to Christmas or birthday gatherings by people they once considered close. The pressure to comply with medical procedures or risk losing jobs, being banned from restaurants, or being excluded from society was overwhelming.

It was both a challenging time and an awakening time, and a time for many people, not just women, had to dig deep to challenge the narrative. For me it was the essence of what strong, clear and unapologetic leadership really means.

I saw during that time so many people re-learn how to trust in themselves when everything around them felt hostile. Question the narrative because it *felt* wrong. Believing in yourself when the whole world seems to be pushing back.

I often reflect on those years and wonder how we made it through without capitulating to the pressure. But out of that pressure came deep, lasting friendships—ones where you could speak your truth freely. Where you felt supported while standing on the precipice, wondering what's next.

And above all, I now see how honouring yourself *with grace* during difficult times is a true act of strength and power.

Our menopausal and midlife journey mirrors this. You are in the process of becoming someone new.

So, while you're facing the challenges of perimenopause, don't put up with symptoms. At this time in your life, *information is power*.

When a woman is informed, she is powerful.

And when a woman honours her emotions, she steps fully into her power.

You might feel as if brain fog is overtaking your day, but trust me, this too shall pass. Your brain is upgrading its operating system. And you *will* come out the other side with more wisdom, sharper intellect, and a refreshing *"I don't give a damn"* attitude. You'll care less about the insignificant, and so much more about what truly matters.

This menopause journey is challenging you to rediscover *you*. To reconnect to the Soul purpose you were born with. Unapologetic Feminine Leadership is your calling and embracing joy and grace during this time is essential. Change doesn't happen in a straight line.

As Gary Vaynerchuk said, *"Change is hard in the beginning, messy in the middle, but glorious at the end."*

There will be days when you're triggered. When your patience is tested. When you wake up and don't want to work out. When that glass of wine or block of chocolate calls your name.

And that's okay.

Because as you begin to clear the limitations, confront the self-sabotage, and release the imposter syndrome, those moments will happen less.

Our shared stories weave themselves into the fabric of how we define ourselves.

In her book *Rising Strong*, Brené Brown writes that stories help us impose order on chaos—including emotional chaos. When we're in pain, we create a narrative to make sense of it.

We all have old stories that shape our identity and beliefs. And whether they're right or wrong, we become *so* invested in them that they feel impossible to change.

From what we say to ourselves, to what we see on social media, these stories are constantly being reaffirmed:

"This is just the way it is."

"I'm just like that."

"I'm not good at that."

"I never get what I want."

"This always happens to me."

Every self-sabotaging habit begins with a story—rooted in an experience from your past.

Something someone said or did, at a moment when you felt vulnerable, planted a seed. A seed you've watered for years with repetition and reinforcement.

And 75% of the thousands of thoughts you have every day are the *same thoughts you had yesterday*—many of them negative, and often self-directed.

Whenever I teach this, I share a concept that helps explain it:

Confirmation Bias.

Confirmation bias is a cognitive tendency to seek out information that confirms what we already believe. Once we've formed a belief, the brain goes into overdrive to prove it's true.

So, it works like this. Let's say you have a secret desire to be an author and have many ideas about writing a book and that's when *Frequency of Illusion* steps in. You start to see ads on social media for masterclasses about how to publish a book. You discover events in your area, where a female guest speaker is an author, who will be sharing her journey about writing her book, and you come across podcasts about women, just like you, who have started new careers after writing their book.

And for a while, it seems, the universe is sending you messages that support your desire to write that book.

Then the little voice in your head starts to create doubt and limitation, as it always does when you start to set those lofty goals. *"Am I smart enough to write a book?" "Who would want to read a book I wrote?" "I'm too busy to write a book" "Who do I think I am anyway."*

Then along comes *Confirmation Bias,* and you start seeing ways to confirm what you really believe about yourself and your capabilities. Suddenly, you read stories of people who have been rejected time and time again by publishers; or authors who have written books that have been highly criticised or judged; or you see books, written by highly successful people, in the $2 reject bin outside the bookstore. Each time you hear another negative story about the challenges authors face, it just confirms to you any negative beliefs you have about your abilities to write that book.

This happens because our brain will always fall back to making those limiting beliefs, the loudest—and subconsciously we avoid anything that might challenge them.

We become emotionally invested in being *right*—because it helps us make sense of the world, and keeps us firmly in our comfort zone, that feels safe.

Once a belief locks in and confirmation bias kicks in, that belief you have about yourself starts showing up everywhere.

We see what we believe, and we speak it out loud, often without even realising it.

The Power of the Words I AM

The words that follow *I am...* follow you. I can't recall where I first heard that phrase—it's been said by many—but it's stuck with me ever since I first heard them

But any time you start a sentence with "I am," you're cementing any belief, and those two little words can either reaffirm an old story... or begin writing a new one.

So, if you want to change your story, start with your *beliefs*. And the fastest way to shift those is through the language you use.

- I am not good at this, change to – I am embracing this new skill with patience.
- I am just getting too old for this, change to – I am wise and experienced.
- I am never going to lose this weight, change to – I am honouring my body and all it has been through.

When you change the *I Am* statements, notice how the changes in the word create a different energy in your body. Words are so powerful, use them wisely.

How to Make Sense of the New Story

In the first tentative weeks of embracing this unapologetic journey, vulnerability is often the most challenging emotion of all.

As you untether from one story and begin to retether to a new one, it can feel shaky—like there's no solid ground. After all, you're not only unlearning everything you once believed about what's possible for you, but you're also rewriting a whole new set of rules—*your* rules.

I remember watching a documentary about earthquakes in New Zealand, where the presenter described a process called *liquefaction*. It occurs when soil under duress— during the shaking of the earth—causes particles to lose contact with one another. As a result, the ground behaves like a liquid and can no longer support weight.

That's exactly what it feels like. The structure of your old story—with all its rigid rules—starts to collapse. You're changing the narrative, but haven't yet created a new, solid foundation.

And because this is not an exact science, the process requires one thing: *belief.*

In those early weeks, you'll question everything.

Especially how rewriting this new story will impact your relationships—particularly those closest to you.

Our primary relationships—parents, partners, close friends—often hold some of our greatest emotional challenges.

When you start rewriting your story, someone will inevitably trigger you. And though it may not feel like a gift in the moment, it is. Because in that moment, you have the opportunity to understand how your past shaped the patterns that still impact your present.

Instead of reacting, get into the habit of asking yourself: **"What is the story I'm telling myself right now?"**

That one question creates a powerful internal dialogue—and brings you closer to understanding *you.*

I shared a story once on my *Isn't It Time* Facebook Live show about how Gerry unintentionally triggered an old wound—over something as simple as punctuation.

I had just spent the entire day creating a landing page for a new program I was launching. I'd researched, written, edited, re-edited, added links, created images, set up email automations—the whole works. By the time I finished, I felt really proud of what I had created.

I asked Gerry to proofread it for me. While he read, I went to the kitchen to pour us both a glass of wine. When I returned, he had already finished reading and moved on to another task. I handed him his wine and asked, *"So, what did you think?"* I was expecting praise. In case you haven't figured it out – my love language is words of affirmation and acts of service!! So, all I wanted to hear was "This is amazing, you are brilliant!"

Instead, without even looking up, he said: *"You have this habit of leaving off full stops."*

Trigger warning. Instant attack mode. *"I didn't ask you about full stops—I asked you what you thought!"*

I was furious. One dismissive sentence felt like it erased all my hard work.

"Why do you always do that?" I snapped. *"Why can't you say it's good first, and then maybe point out a few grammar things? Do you know I haven't even stopped for lunch? I've been up since 4 am!"*

He was lucky I'd already put the glass of wine down—otherwise, I might have thrown it.

He looked up, confused, and simply said, *"It's OK, I fixed them."*

I stormed off. But then I stopped myself. *"Okay, Ms. Mid-life Coach—what is the story you're telling yourself right now?"*

So, I sat down in the living room and started tapping. Furiously at first, I was still cranky!

Not even halfway through a round of EFT, a memory came flooding back.

My Grade 5 end-of-year report: 10/10 for Creative Writing. 5/10 for Grammar and Punctuation. With a note from Mother Columba: *"Sally is a lovely little creative writer, but she needs to focus more on grammar and punctuation."*

I can't remember the story I wrote, but I do remember being proud of it—and devastated that I didn't win the English prize because of the grammar mark.

Suddenly, I saw it. Gerry's comment had triggered that belief:

"My writing isn't good enough." And deeper than that: **"I'm not good enough."**

His offhand remark wasn't what upset me. What hurt was my 10-year-old self still carrying the injustice of that moment.

Years ago, that would've led to an entire night of silence, coupled with a packet of corn chips devoured with a giant bowl of guacamole.

But now, I have the tools to catch myself. (Though asking "What's the story I'm telling myself?" *before* storming off, is still a work in progress!)

Here's the truth: when you're triggered by someone, it's not about *them*. It's about *you*. And that trigger is an invitation to uncover the stories from your past that are still quietly shaping your life.

Success isn't about changing who you are. It's about reclaiming who you were before the world told you otherwise.

You don't need to change yourself. Your only responsibility is to release the emotional weight of the memory that's keeping you stuck.

We can't change the past—but we *can* release its emotional grip. And that gives us the freedom to rewrite a different future.

Gerry triggered my old belief that what I do is never good enough. It's not true. It's just a story I've told myself—and one I'm choosing to rewrite.

When something matters deeply, that's when your limiting beliefs come up loud and clear. That's just how it works.

The higher the intention, the greater the vulnerability. Why? Because there's more at stake.

No one wants to fail publicly. So instead, we often choose to fail privately—quietly backing away, so no one notices.

If I hadn't cleared that emotional charge around full stops, it would have shown up in other ways. I would have set up that self-sabotaging behaviour that would have stopped me from probably finishing this book.

This is the same reason we don't apply for the job, post the video, or speak up when it matters. We fail privately... because it feels safer.

But the truth is, the answer doesn't lie in the food you don't eat, the job you don't go for, or the video you avoid recording.

It lies deep within the pain of your 4-year-old self...
Your 10-year-old self...
Your 16-year-old self...
...who once felt like she just wasn't enough.

Rewriting the story of your life starts *now*.

This powerful midlife chapter is your time. Uncovering and releasing your old story is part of the journey. And yes, the ground will feel shaky. The soil might feel liquefied. But once you cross that threshold... The view is breathtaking!

Confidence Is an Inside Job

"Okay, Sally, I get the part about listening to your intuition—but how do you find the confidence to trust yourself? What if you are wrong?"

It was a question asked by one of the participants midway through the last day of a two-day seminar.

As soon as she spoke, you could have heard a pin drop. After all the inner work and breakthroughs, they'd been experiencing, it was clear this question resonated with everyone in the room.

I took my time before answering.

And finally said,

"The problem for most of us, is that we think confidence is a personality trait. It's not. Confidence, like courage, comes from moving out of fear and inertia and into action. But the challenge is, many of us grew up in a time when there were more expectations than dreams.

We were told what to do and how to think. The rules were strict, and they didn't encourage us to make our own choices—let alone trust them.

To lead unapologetically, we must unlearn the rules we've carried for years. Because those rules defined us. We didn't need confidence to make our own decisions—there was always a rule to follow.

That's why you need to give yourself time on this journey. Time to develop confidence. This isn't a rule-bound process. It's a journey of choices."

When I first began practicing intuitive eating, that was one of the biggest challenges for me. Letting go of rules about dieting and weight loss felt like going against everything I'd ever believed. I had to find the confidence to trust myself again.

I grew up believing that being a 'good girl' meant doing the right thing, being accepted, and fitting in. There were so many unspoken rules—about behaviours, beliefs, and appearance—that you rarely questioned what you were doing or why.

I was educated in a Catholic girls' school by nuns who did not encourage us to think for ourselves or speak our minds.

We spent more time being lectured about dress length, wearing hats, confessing our sins, and avoiding boys, than we did learning how to trust our own decisions.

My world was bound by antiquated rules. Girls were to be quiet and demure. You had to show utmost respect to those in authority—no matter how poorly they treated you. And above all, you never questioned that authority.

When I was 14, I was hit by a nun with a broom—so hard I fell off the platform at the front of the classroom. My crime? Not knowing the answer to a maths question. And yet, as she walked out of the room, we were still expected to curtsey to her. If that doesn't send confusing signals about what's right and wrong—or who gets to decide—I don't know what does.

We were told that if you spoke up, you were insolent. If you wore your dress too short, you were destined for ruin. And if you left school without your hat and gloves, you were 'sending the wrong message.'

It's a wonder we're still functioning.

All of these external messages get imprinted at a cellular level. I remember once joking with a fellow former Catholic EFT practitioner: *"We could open any page of our catechism book... and just start tapping."*

We often unconsciously live by that strict set of rules that were part of our upbringing. Whether those rules make any sense or not, we handed over our ability to decide what's right for *us* to someone we thought knew better than us.

Why? Because that's what we were taught. That's how we adapted.

I once had a client who was struggling to trust herself—both at work and in her personal life. She was incredibly capable in her leadership role, but she carried a secret she hadn't told anyone:

"I have real issues believing I can do this," she said. *"Every time you talk about authenticity, I get a knot in my stomach. I'm in a new relationship with a great guy... but honestly, what terrifies me is the thought that if I gain weight, he'll leave me. I'm so confident at work, but that... that scares the hell out of me."*

And there it was.

She named the quiet truth many women carry: our confidence is often eroded by deep-rooted beliefs about our body and worth.

We learn early—often from our parents—how we're supposed to act in order to feel loved and safe.

As children we relied on learning how to act in the world, by watching the adults in our lives. Our parents, teachers or mentors, who show us how to act, speak, and be. But when the messages are mixed or shaming, it's no wonder so many of us grew up unsure of where we fit or what our boundaries even were.

And even now, women are still struggling to find their confidence. Except now it's not parents, nuns and priests—it's social media and mainstream media, who set the standards of how women should look, and often act—especially in mid-life!

It is extraordinary that in 2025, women in leadership are still critically judged by how old they look, the colour of their hair, or the clothes they wear. And that can so easily chip away at your confidence.

Will it ever change? I don't think so. We can give lip-service to it, but in the coaching, I have done over the years, it is the one thing many women really struggle with.

The thing is, we can talk about 'them' changing, but the reality is, 'they' won't. We must be the change.

By being the living breathing example of what we believe. Being open in questioning yourself about what you really believe about yourself throughout this ageing process. Building your confidence by *being in motion,* being clear in your vision, and taking daily action towards that vision, and re-learning to trust in yourself.

Start by identifying the moment in your past when your confidence was first shaken.

For me, that moment came at nine years old.

One of my favourite nuns, Sister Helen, asked me to sing at the front of the class. I had no idea why she chose me, but I was a confident, sassy little thing back then. I loved singing and I loved the ceremony of church. So up I went, hands clasped, eyes cast upward, trying to look as angelic as I could. (I would have made a great actress—or a great nun! Both were on my radar at the time.)

Later that day, Sister Helen gave me a letter to take home to my mum. When Mum read it, she beamed with pride. The letter said I had the voice of an angel and asked if I would sing at the school concert the following week.

I was thrilled. But that changed quickly.

Another girl, Suzanne, was also singing. She was older— maybe 16—and she had the voice of an opera singer. I listened to her and thought, *I can't compete with that.*

I walked onto the stage trembling. I'd chosen a song I loved singing at home—*Three Little Fishies.* But when I opened my mouth, my mind went blank. I stumbled through the words and hummed to the chorus: *"Boop boop dit-tem dat-tem what-tem Chu!"*

The older girls in the audience started sniggering. I was mortified.

So, I tried to cover it with more animation—gestures that worked at home with my little sisters. But in front of older girls? It just made things worse. They laughed harder.

I sat down, humiliated. My moment of glory was gone. My nine-year-old self felt like a total failure.

That moment became frozen in my subconscious. The feeling of embarrassment... the sound of laughter... it stuck.

Years later, even when I was teaching a fitness class to over 2,000 people, that memory still haunted me. The fear of forgetting the words. Of looking stupid. Of being laughed at.

It robbed me of enjoying those moments. After a major event, instead of celebrating, I'd be picking myself apart – wondering if I looked silly or if I could've done better.

It impacted so many opportunities in my life. I turned down invitations. Looked for ways to avoid stepping into the spotlight.

In the lead-up to that big aerobics event, I lived on rice crackers and low-fat cottage cheese. If I was going to mess up, at least I'd be skinny!

Looking back now—especially watching the footage my daughter found recently, deep in the archives of CBC TV. I can see it. I wasn't confident. I was *trying* to be.

I even remember worrying how my bum looked... and then seeing it on the front page of the newspaper, I could pick apart everything that was wrong, instead of focusing on that incredible achievement.

The journey back to reclaiming the confidence I had at nine was not easy. But once I uncovered that old memory, and released the emotional charge, everything shifted.

That fear no longer holds me back.

Now, I don't believe I need to be a certain size or shape to follow my dreams. I trust my intuition. And the confidence I feel in this post-menopausal chapter of life is *real*.

That memory is still there—but it no longer controls me.

Clawing back your confidence, day by day, to reclaim the real you? It's nothing short of liberating.

The Power of Forgiveness

One of the most powerful gifts we can give ourselves, is the practise of forgiveness, of ourselves and of others.

This time in your life is about writing a new story–a story rewritten by choosing to release the emotional pain and regret of your past.

While EFT and meditation are great for doing that, the simple practise of forgiving what we have done and what has been done to us in the past, is so powerful, liberating and above all joyful.

Every infraction that still holds a charge for us, holds us back from that joy.

One of the most powerful tools of forgiveness I have ever come across is the practice of **Ho'oponopono** (ho-o-pono-pono), an ancient Hawaiian method of reconciliation and forgiveness, made famous by Clinical Psychologist Dr. Ihaleakala Hew Len and brought to wider popularity by Dr. Joe Vitale in his book *Zero Limits*.

Dr. Hew Len's story is extraordinary. He reportedly healed an entire ward of criminally insane inmates in Hawaii, so much so that they were all released and the ward was eventually shut down. But he did so, without ever meeting them in person— only through the practice of Ho'oponopono. He would simply hold the file of each of the inmates while saying the words *"I'm sorry, I love you, please forgive me, thankyou"* This practise honours the belief that by taking personal responsibility for your own reality, believing that everything in life is a reflection of your inner state and acknowledge your part in any situation, even if it seems external. His story shows that forgiveness can be an incredibly powerful force to release pain and suffering *within ourselves*.

While it seems almost impossible, the work of Dr Len is renowned and while not as extreme as his story, I have witnessed some incredible results from people who have used this practice in their own lives. From healing relationships with estranged family members, overcoming trauma and everything in between.

When we forgive others, and ourselves, for the role we played in any situation, we create space for healing. And forgiveness is something we can practice *every single day*.

Why is this important in midlife—and in leadership?

You cannot fully step into strong, clear, and unapologetic leadership if you do are hanging on to past hurts or emotions. You are a divine, intuitive being and being stuck in anger, regret, resentment or sadness, stops you from expressing the wholeness of your true leadership.

The thing is, that forgiveness is not about accepting the behaviour of others, it is about releasing you from the emotional restraints, so you are free.

In 1986, in Australia, a young woman, Anita Cobby, was abducted on her way home from work by five men. Over many hours she was raped and brutalized multiple times before being murdered. It was a shocking crime that rocked Australia.

A few years later, her father was interviewed on a lunchtime talk show. He said *"I couldn't let go, I was so angry for so many years, until one day my niece said to me "Uncle, your feeling towards those men is making no difference in their lives, but they are destroying yours. It was at that moment; I chose to forgive them for what they did – and it changed my life".*

I have never forgotten that moment. If somebody could forgive a crime like that done to his daughter, what a difference it would make in all of our lives, if we practised forgiveness for everything and everybody that has caused us pain in the past.

You are where you are today because of all the good, and not so good, circumstances that happened to you in the past. Choosing to release any hurt and pain of the past, forgiving it and moving on, frees you up to live a more joy-filled life.

You'll begin to feel more alive, more vibrant. You'll look younger. Because as the weight of pain, anger hurt and shame lifts, your radiance begins to return.

But talk is cheap — action is where transformation happens.

Just like an apology means little without changed behaviour, forgiveness must be followed by *different choices*.

So now, after forgiving yourself, your next step is to honour yourself through *action*.

That means every decision you make for you, comes from a place of self-love. From honouring the extraordinary miracle that is you and *your* body.

It's about listening to your body's cues—especially in the menopausal transition.

Eat food that supports your vitality and nourishes the elegant, sensual, powerful woman that you are. Move your body as if it is the most expensive thing you can buy. Choose supplements and skin care that enhance your energy and vibrance. Take time to rest, to restore and to rejuvenate.

It's not about being perfect—it's about choosing wisely *most* of the time.

This is the only body you get. You don't get a second one.

How you treat it today determines how it will support you for the next 10, 20, 30 or 50 years. The decisions you make *now* are your insurance policy for the life ahead.

Forgiving Yourself—for the Next Generation

I've been having this conversation since my kids were small.

Nearly every woman I've coached has said some version of:
"I don't want my daughter to grow up with the same limiting beliefs that I had, about what I could achieve in my life, or pass on negative thoughts about my body"

What began as a conversation about body image and confidence has now also become a mission to educate our daughters—*and sons*—about hormones, perimenopause, and menopause and what is possible in mid-life.

Almost every midlife woman I speak with tells me the same thing:

"My mother never talked about menopause."

Think about that. *Fifty-one percent* of the global population will go through it—and yet, most of us had no roadmap.

This stops with us.

We are the mentors, the mothers, the grandmothers, the aunties, the leaders. It's *our* job to speak the truth. To educate and empower the next generation *before* they need it.

It's up to us to change the narrative. To break the silence. To lead—strong, clear, and unapologetically.

Because let's be honest, life is already hard for our kids today. They're growing up with constant pressure: Be successful. Be beautiful. Be forever young.

We didn't have Instagram filters in the '70s and '80s. We didn't have anti-wrinkle ads popping up every time we opened our phones. Our teenage years were free from the constant barrage of information.

But if we want to see change, we must *be* the change.

That means:

- Advocating for menopause education in the workplace—for men and women.

- Challenging outdated medical perspectives.

- Creating safe, empowered spaces to talk, share, and lead.

- Being the living breathing example of what we say and teach.

Midlife women are the most powerful, wise, and insightful leaders of our time. And yes, we *can* change the story.

But it starts with one woman at a time. One leader. One decision.

One choice to reclaim her body, her power, and her voice.

It is entirely possible that many of us in our 40's, 50s and 60s will live to 100 and beyond. So—how do you want those years to look?

The decisions you make today, are your investment in the decades to come.

This journey—of being strong, clear, and unapologetic... of reclaiming your body and reclaiming *you*... starts right now.

This is the first step in the rest of your most extraordinary life.

Are you ready?

A number of years ago, I participated in a 17-kilometre bushwalk with a group of good friends.

It was an enjoyable, yet often challenging, day—and as we made our way along the track, I couldn't help noticing how closely it mirrored the journey of choosing to embrace stronger, leaner, unapologetic leadership.

The decision to go on the hike was met with great enthusiasm in the lead-up. There was lots of planning, questions, organization, anticipation—and a little doubt.

While it seemed like fun at first, as the day drew closer, a few people in the group began to question whether they could really complete it. Whether they had signed up for something they weren't quite sure they were capable of.

Excitement was high as we set off, but the path ahead brought more challenges than expected.

Although we knew our starting point and destination, the route was not as straightforward as we imagined.

Some sections were easy to navigate, but much of the track required close attention—tree roots, muddy and slippery patches, uneven terrain, and no guardrails to catch us if we stumbled. In places, one wrong step could've meant falling down a steep ravine.

We crossed several creeks that demanded care and precision. Some of us got across with no problem, others needed support, and a few, despite our best efforts, ended up with wet shoes and socks.

In the final two kilometres, exhaustion started to kick in. Some people were dealing with blisters, others with stiff legs. A few chose to slow down to support those who needed it. Others sped up to relieve the growing discomfort in their muscles.

But in the end, *everyone* reached the destination— blisters, sore legs, and muddy backpacks included.

And you know what we all said when we gathered in the bar at the end? *"Let's plan another one."*

Despite the setbacks, despite the struggle, we were proud of what we had achieved. The beauty of the waterfalls, the joy of completion, the camaraderie—we felt it all.

That's what this journey is like.

You make the decision because something in you says yes. And yes, there will be moments of doubt. There will be days when it feels easy—when you can breathe deeply, be present, and enjoy the view.

And there will be days when it's hard. When you're crossing emotional creeks, navigating unstable ground, or feeling like one wrong step might send you tumbling.

But like our bushwalk, once you begin, there's no turning back. And you won't *want* to. Even in the toughest moments, you'll find the strength—or the support—to keep going.

It won't matter who gets there first or last. What matters is that you *get there*.

At the start of the trail that day was a sign that read: **"Take only photos, leave only footprints."**

That's what this journey is about.

To embrace unapologetic leadership is to walk through the emotional limitations of your past with compassion— taking the memories but leaving behind the weight of the beliefs that no longer serve you.

You are where you are now because of every belief you've ever held about yourself.

And now that you're ready to change, every single limiting belief will rise to the surface. That's not failure. That's the process.

This path has no rules. Some women will move quickly, others more slowly. Some will receive help along the way. Others will slip, even with support.

That's just how it goes.

But knowing that from the outset helps make the harder days more bearable.

Take it one day at a time. Stay present. Keep your eye on the destination—and still enjoy the journey... blisters and all.

And for those of you who are tempted to implement *every single strategy* in this book at once—then panic when it doesn't go perfectly, and spiral into self-doubt— please... I see you. I *am* you.

But don't do that. Take this journey *one step at a time*.

There are no hard and fast rules here. What works for me may not work for you. And that's okay.

Be kind to yourself. Be gentle. Be gracious.

Give yourself a break.

Some days, I don't get it right either. I spend too much time on social media. As I write this, my desk looks like a cyclone passed through it. And there are still days when I walk into a room and can't remember why, or those mornings when my sleep hasn't gone according to plan and I choose to stay an extra hour in bed, rather than hitting gym.

But that's the beauty of this menopausal journey. There will be days you absolutely nail it. And days you won't.

The journey doesn't end on those days. The goal is not to stay stuck there. When a "not-so-great" day happens, turn to one of the 10 Principles. Ask yourself: **"Which one do I need to focus on today?"**

Maybe it's *Exercise Purposefully*. Maybe it's *Forgive Easily*. One will call to you. Trust that.

That's what self-actualization is.

Not getting it perfect—but getting *closer to this new version of yourself* each day.

And let's be honest: perfection is overrated. That's why I still enjoy a wine or a glass of bubbles on a Friday night. I exercise regularly, eat intuitively, and I'm in the best physical shape of my life.

I meditate, visualize, practice gratitude, and journal most days. It's what allows me to feel grounded, joyful, and expansive.

And if I didn't have that glass of something I enjoy... well, I'd be boring. And I'd have no friends left! (That's my story, and I'm sticking to it.)

This menopausal journey— is not an exact science and can feel like a rollercoaster ride. Your journey is unique. One woman going through menopause – is one woman going through menopause. For each of us, our journey is different. No right or wrong, just different.

When you honour the changes in your body and brain— without comparison, judgement, or apology—you reclaim your power. When you give yourself permission to seek solutions, advocate fiercely for your wellbeing, and refuse to simply endure, you rise. And when you commit to the inner work of reframing the beliefs that have held you back, you unlock the path home to yourself. Commit to this, and you won't just navigate midlife—you will rise through it, reclaiming the sensual, energetic, powerful, intuitive woman you are. Strong. Clear. Unapologetic.

Appendix

Emotional Freedom Techniques (EFT)

In this appendix is some more information that may help you if you have not come across Emotional Freedom Techniques (Tapping) before.

The history of EFT started simply enough. Originally developed by Psychologist Dr Roger Callahan who discovered tapping whilst working with a patient with a severe water phobia, and his original version is known as Thought Field Therapy today.

One of his students, Gary Craig, began experimenting with tapping and simplified the procedure, which later became the version of EFT widely used today.

Clinical trials have shown that tapping is able to rapidly reduce the emotional impact of memories and incidents that trigger emotional distress.

It works by lowering cortisol levels. A randomized controlled study by Dr Dawson Church and his team focused on changes to cortisol levels in 83 subjects. They were separated into three groups - one used EFT, another conventional therapy and the final group received no treatment.

The final group and the conventional therapy group showed only a 14 % drop in cortisol over time. While the

EFT group showed a 24 % decrease, some experiencing up to 50%.

It appears that once distress or stress is reduced or removed; the body can often rebalance itself and accelerate healing.

Today, EFT has been shown to be effective for anxiety, stress, pain, phobias and many others. It is a simple technique that in essence helps lower your stress levels, so you are able to think clearly.

How to Tap

Whilst there are now many versions of tapping available, I prefer to use what is commonly known as Clinical EFT. Simply because the majority of the studies mentioned before, involved the use of this particular method.

First let's look at the 9 tapping points now used in the clinical version of EFT.

1. **Side of Hand point** – with two fingers, tap the side of your other hand where you would do a "karate chop". In the book I refer to this as the **Set Up Statement** as you'll see in the script below.

The points then work in sequence (tapping on each point about 4 – 8 times).

EB = Eyebrow Point – where the hair of the eyebrow meets the nose.

SE = Side of the Eye – follow the bone around the eye socket and tap.

UE = Under the Eye – Again follow the bone of the eye socket and tap under the eye, directly under the pupil.

UN = Under the nose.

Chin = The groove in just below the lips, but above the chin bone itself.

CB = Collar bone point. Find where the collar bone meets the centre of your chest, drop down a little and you will feel the fleshy part just under the collar bone.

UA = Under the arm. About 4 inches from the arm pit, or where the bra strap would sit for a woman.

TH = Top of the head – Right in the centre of the skull.

You can tap with one hand, both hands and whichever side is comfortable for you. In tapping there is no 'right and wrong' – simply what feels right for you.

Telling the Truth and Being Specific

EFT's great power, I believe, comes from our ability to connect to our own truth. All too often we are not encouraged to tell the truth about how we feel. We are encouraged to think positively, often ignoring our true emotions.

For many clients, the 'telling the truth' part is often the first time they have actually voiced how they really felt about an issue. Those beliefs, thoughts and words buried deep within our subconscious. The ones that we don't often want to admit to having.

There is no political correctness in EFT – it is how YOU feel, what YOU think, and nobody will judge you or try to sugar coat it for you. Whatever YOU feel, is right for you! The quality of the words you use, getting as close as you can to how you are really feeling, will create a more powerful outcome.

In fact, in order for EFT to work effectively, you need to state what emotion and feeling as best you can. Being too general won't clear the belief.

As an example, if you want to tap on dealing with your weight - rather than just saying..."*Even though I don't like my weight the way it is*", a more specific statement would be to say, *"Even though, the thought of putting on a bikini and walking onto the beach makes me feel so embarrassed, because I have gained 10 kilos and I just feel fat and I hate myself"*. That's the truth part. It doesn't make you right or wrong... it's just the truth for you.

People telling you to love yourself when you don't, will not make you love yourself – no matter how many times you say it!

How To Use The Tapping Scripts and Videos.

You can access many tapping scripts in my first book Tapping to Reclaim You, or head to my website www.sallythibault.com.au to be able to access a free version of a tapping video.

Whilst tapping scripts and videos are somewhat 'generalized', tapping is most powerful when you are specific as you can be about what you are feeling.

The more specific you can get to the memory of where the first time you experienced the event that caused some form or trauma or emotion, that formed the belief you now have, the faster you will be able to release a pattern and change the way you experience life.

Many people have lost the art of being in touch with their emotions and feelings – a critical aspect to Intuitive Eating.

Whether that has been through conditioning – growing up in a family where emotion was considered a weakness or learning at a young age how to disconnect from your emotions in order to feel safe. This can cause an emotional disconnect.

Our body will reflect what is going on for us emotionally, whether we like to believe it or not!

Most physical issues have an emotional connection. You are not unhappy because you are overweight, you are overweight because you are unhappy, stressed, angry, frustrated, hurt or any other emotion you experience.

That's the power of EFT and the art of intuitive eating, it helps you understand that what you are feeling may have an emotional connection.

You may experience a headache if you are feeling stressed; a sore lower back if you are feeling unsupported; feeling tiredness if you are overwhelmed.

Many of the discomforts we feel, may come from an emotion or a belief we have ignored.

The problem is that many people either put up with the discomfort or choose to take medication instead, rather than first examining if there is an emotional reason behind it.

Our body is like our early warning system. It lets you know when something isn't right, but many people have become disconnected from the 'mind' that exists within our body.

EFT helps you reconnect to the way your body feels. Allowing you to become very adept at knowing when something doesn't feel right. At the same time uncovering the reason for the pain, or the emotion you feel and sometimes even healing it!

We always begin with a Set-Up Statement, tapping on the Side of Hand point. And we say the words *"Even though.... I have this issue going on... I deeply and completely accept myself and how I feel"* In other words – even though I have this issue going on, I am fine! It's just an issue, and I accept that this is how I feel.

Before using EFT with any client, the first thing I ask is *"What emotion are you feeling?"* and *"Where in your body do you feel it?"* followed by *"What is the earliest memory you have where you remember feeling this?"* When people first start tapping, some struggle with the concept of 'finding the feeling', but after a while, they become attuned to their own bodies.

That is the key indicator in *Intuitive Eating*. You have to *feel* what your body really wants and needs. To get out of your head (which has caused the problem in the first place) and connect to the feeling in your body.

Your body knows. It knows. When you don't listen to the knowledge that is held within your body and allow your brain to make the bigger decisions, that is where the disconnect starts.

Your intuition is the most powerful emotion you will ever experience – if you give yourself permission to listen.

EFT gets you back in touch with what the real emotion is, where it is, and helps you understand the cause behind it.

There are no random thoughts or emotions. Every single though and emotion has a root cause. In order to understand and release the emotional connection to your thoughts and subsequently the beliefs that really do not serve you – your role is to find the root cause.

Where did it start? What emotional connection are you carrying? What triggers those responses? And for the purpose of this book – how do those triggers impact on your body?

This is where working with an experienced EFT Coach is really powerful. An experienced EFT coach will be able to guide you to get to the root cause of the emotion. In my experience this is the most challenging aspects of working with EFT, as often you cannot hear the words you are saying. An EFT coach knows how to ask the right questions.

You can find many of my tapping videos on my You Tube account – www.youtube.com/sallythibault.

EFT is one of the fastest methods I know that will help you answer all those questions, in a safe, non-threatening way.

How Often Do You Need To Tap?

EFT is like exercise for your beliefs! A routine that forms part of your daily habits, just like exercise or meditation.

It is not a standalone practise, but a way of living. I suggest to clients to use EFT any time they have a disempowering thought or a feeling. Those pesky negative confirmation bias thoughts often referred to as 'tailenders', which cause doubt or fear in your mind.

But, like exercise, tapping works well if it is done every day, or, at least, two to three times per week.

Our beliefs about ourselves are often supported by various aspects. Gary Craig referred to our issues as Tabletops, supported by various aspects, like Table Legs. The table legs may be all sorts of events, words or emotions, from the past that combine to form a belief.

What we believe to be true for us, is supported by a core belief that may have, at its heart, an event/s, a person/people or a word/s that caused us pain in the past. Until we deal with each one of those emotions, events or issues we will continue to recreate the same patterns in our lives that come from that belief.

For example, perhaps you always procrastinate when you have a big project or goal you want to achieve. Leaving everything till the last minute and then completing the task quickly and haphazardly to eventually get it done. It doesn't matter how important the project is, or how badly you want to complete it, you always have trouble starting and completing the task and continually find ways to be distracted.

You may even use words such as *"I always do this"*, or *"No matter how hard I try I always leave things to the last minute, and it's never good enough."*

The way to change the habit is to not focus on the procrastination (the tabletop), rather to examine the times your emotions, thoughts or feelings cause you to procrastinate. (the table legs).

Perhaps completing the task means that you will be successful and that feels scary for you. Perhaps there was an event in your past where you were successful, and people challenged or criticised you. Perhaps there was a person in your past who told you that you were not worthy of success. Perhaps you were once told that you would never amount to anything in your life. Or perhaps all of them!

The procrastination is simply a way to keep you safe from experiencing the pain of the past. It is the way your brain reiterates what you believe to be true about yourself. In order to totally overcome the habit of procrastination you need to find all the 'aspects' (table legs) that keep you continuing with that behaviour (table top). Sometimes you can tap and release all the aspects in one go; sometimes it takes a little longer. But if you still do it... you haven't cleared it!

Nothing we do is ever random. There is always a reason behind all our behaviours – the good and the not so good. If you have a pattern or a habit that you want to change in your life you can. Simply by being mindful of your thoughts and feelings and tapping to uncover and release the cause of the belief in the first place.

Is It Magic?

I am not sure about calling EFT magic – but there are some outcomes that I have trouble explaining!

There are two things that seem to happen in tapping. One is a physiological impact and the other... well, perhaps it is magic after all!

The Physiological Part

EFT appears to calm the emotional response by deactivating the brain's arousal pathways.

The amygdala of our brain – an almond-shaped set of neurons located deep in the brain's medial temporal lobe - plays a key role is processing our emotions. It helps keep us safe by helping to stimulate our flight, fight or freeze response. If, as a child, you touched a hot stove and burnt your hand, the amygdala's part in the process is to stop you doing that again.

But the amygdala can also stop us from moving past the pain and trauma of the past, instead causing us to relive it over and over again, and then rewiring a new pattern that is designed to keep us safe but trapped in the repeating pattern.

For instance, extra weight could be masking a fear of public speaking that could then stem from the time you fell over in the playground and everybody laughed at you. Anxiety and fear causing you to feel high levels of fear every time you are required to speak in public - reminding you that if you slip up, people might laugh at you. Your weight becomes the physical response to that, and the story you tell yourself.

"When I am 10kg lighter, I will feel better about speaking in public" or "I need to lose these few extra kilos so I can fit into my power outfit, and I will feel more confident."

The beliefs we have about our body, are simply old stories we keep telling ourselves, to keep us from dealing with the real issues.

We are the total of all the trauma, fears or emotions of our past, which are simply playing out as patterns in our present.

EFT helps to calm our emotional responses to an event then reduces the flight, fight or freeze response, allowing rational, wisdom based, calm thought to return. This effectively clears trauma and emotion caused from experiences of your past and creates new ways of believing for your new future!

The Magic Part

One of my favourite sayings is *"In order for things to change, first I must change"*, and in EFT, this is the absolute truth.

Many of my clients tell me that when they tap on something that drives them crazy about somebody else – magically that person seems to stop doing whatever it was that drove them crazy!

The issue is never about the other person. It is always about us. When we take 100% responsibility for our reactions, we can release the emotional intensity we have to the behaviours of others.

What we think and feel creates energy that reflects outwards from us and in doing so creates who, or what, we attract into our lives. Tapping on what we feel suddenly changes that.

What I have seen over and over again however is difficult to explain. I have worked with clients who are worried or upset about a child's behaviour, tap on how that behaviour makes them feel and within days that child stops exhibiting that behaviour! I have also had clients who have tapped on how a boss or a co-worker treats them that makes them feel stressed or frustrated – to then have that boss or co-worker suddenly treat them as if they were their best friend!

As we tap on how we feel about something and shift the intensity of that feeling or emotion, we change. Our vibrational energy changes and lifts. When that happens, people change how they respond to us and we change how we respond to them.

When you tap and clear the limiting beliefs and patterns that are holding you back, it is as if the true magic of who you are and what you are truly capable of experiencing unfolds.

The Reframe Reclaim Round

At the end of every tapping script is what I call the **Reframe Reclaim Round.** A powerful way to recreate a new way of believing, thinking, acting and manifesting.

I developed the process after using different versions of a number of modalities with clients over time. The modalities include the work of Dr Patricia Carrington, Dr Joe Dispenza, Dr Hew Lenn, Dr Joe Vitale, Karl Dawson, Professor Amy Cuddy and others.

I created the *Reframe Reclaim Round* on the language that resonates most powerfully with our feminine wisdom. To create a strong vision for what you do want, requires a level of belief, before it becomes reality. Or as Professor Amy Cuddy in her viral Ted Talk said "To fake it until you become it!"

So, this final round is to create a powerful vision, backed up with a strong mantra. Used with EFT to rewire a new way of believing. Just like that mantra I said over and over again almost four decades ago. Only this time, I am also 'tapping' it into being. But the Reframe Reclaim Round will not work, unless you use the tapping sequence first.

After you feel all the aspects of an issue have been dealt with and you feel a 0 – 2 level of intensity; it is then you that you can move onto the *Reframe Reclaim Round* – but not before! Otherwise, it's like putting on a band-aid on a cut, without using a disinfectant first. It might look good for the moment, but it's not going to help that cut heal!

To begin the Reframe Reclaim Round, first create detailed clear picture about what you want to manifest in your life. So while you are imagining it, it is important to feel it. What does that emotion feel like. Dr Joe Dispenza in his book, *You Are The Placebo*, says that if you want to change a belief or perception, you have to first change your state of being. You cannot change your reality, if you do not have a strong vision of what you now want.

Then to ask the question of yourself *"What do I need most to create this outcome?"*

Your intuition will always provide you with just the right answers. It is then we can go back to a time in your past and tap on healing that moment.

Each of the scripts then has three elements...

The first is *Choice*. Originally developed by Dr Patricia Carrington in her work with EFT when she realized that for many people affirmations were a huge challenge.

That is why I get so frustrated with people who talk about using affirmations only as a way to change.

They are not! They will help reinforce the belief once you have changed it at that cellular brain level, but just saying a sentence over and over again won't work, unless you are prepared to do the inner work., perhaps you have been trying to say an affirmation like" *I love and accept my body"*, or *"I am my perfect body every way."* How does that feel when you do that? Does it resonate for you?

And last question..." How is that working for you?"

In my experience, the reality and continuing to say something that seems so far out of your grasp right now can feel overwhelming and daunting.

However, when you change that to say *"I choose to believe it is possible to have my perfect for me body"* or, of course our most powerful one for Reclaiming your body, *"I choose to listen to my body and honour the messages I hear"*, the emphasis returns to your power. It's a proactive way to instill a new belief that you believe will eventually come to fruition... because you have chosen it!

In the Reframe Reclaim Round, we are powerfully stating what you now choose to believe, because first you have tapped to release the pattern that created the job you hated in the first place! Now YOU are deciding what you will now create! It's fun and a little bit exciting at the same time. Starting with a blank slate and putting the power of choice right back in your own hands.

Next is to add a statement of gratitude for your intention— even if it is yet to be there.

The second is *Forgiveness.* Forgiveness of yourself and of others is the way to free yourself from the confines of thoughts and emotions that simply do not serve you.

Then finally at the end of the *Reframe Reclaim Round,* you will have the opportunity to powerfully lock in the new belief, using a *power pose* with a powerful intention statement.

The *power pose* is based on research by Social Psychologist and Harvard Professor Amy Cuddy whose research showed that by assuming a 'power pose' (think Wonder women, with hands on hips and legs planted firmly on the ground) can increase the hormone testosterone by as much as 20% and at the same time reduce cortisol by as much as 25%. (You can learn more about the pose from Amy's famous 2012 Ted Talk – Your Body Language Shapes Who You Are).

What was interesting in her research was that this physiological change actually impacted biochemically with 86% of power posers reporting that they felt more likely to take chances. Compared to those who stood in more passive poses (arms and legs crossed and a more slumped posture) where their testosterone levels dropped by 10% and cortisol levels rose by 15%!

Notwithstanding that posture and core strength are aspects we will be dealing with later in this book, as we sit more now than ever before, not only can the *power pose* increase your confidence – but it can also improve your posture! Making you look more powerful (even if you are yet to feel it!)

Many clients have reported that adopting the *power pose* alone, before an important meeting has enabled them to stay focused and clear. In fact, one of my clients reported that prior to a sales meeting with a previously difficult client, she first tapped on her feelings of apprehension, then adopted the power pose in her mind. The sales meeting went better than she expected, with her client greeting her warmly and giving her an order that she had not expected.

There are many different versions of the *Reframe Reclaim Round*, dependent on the issue you are facing. In fact, when I am working with clients, there is actually no script to follow. It's very fluid, based on what the client tells me.

I have experienced some powerful *Reframe Reclaim Rounds* not only for my clients, but also for myself. Like a re-setting a new way of thinking and a whole new way of manifesting what you want in your life. You just experience life differently!

A Word of Caution

Often times it is difficult to clear a block on your own. Tapping works by being as specific as you can, and sometimes that can be difficult. That's where a suitably qualified professional or certified EFT practitioner can help.

Tapping To Become An Intuitive Eater.

As an example of how EFT can work, below is a tapping script. (A version of this is also available on my YouTube channel - https://www.youtube.com/@SallyThibault

First, ask yourself *"What if I believed it was possible for me to become an Intuitive Eater?" "What if I allowed myself to totally trust my intuition to make the choices?"*

Now measure the *feeling* in your body when you ask the question.

Is there a feeling of fear? Could you trust yourself? Is there a feeling of disbelief that it couldn't possibly work? Whatever the thought or feeling, write it down.

Where do you *feel* the emotion? Then measure the level of intensity on a scale of 1-10 (10 being the highest intensity) and write it down.

Let's start tapping:

Set-Up Statement: Even though when I think of the possibility of embracing intuitive eating, I feel this fear, I deeply and completely accept myself and how I feel.

Set-Up Statement: Even though I have this (intensity number) feeling in my (where in your body) about the thought of allowing my body and intuition to make the choice, and it makes me feel (emotion), I deeply and completely accept myself and how I feel.

Set-Up Statement: Even though I have this (emotion) feeling in my (where in your body) whenever I think about just trusting my intuition to make the choices, I am scared I might put on weight, I deeply and completely accept myself and how I feel.

EB: This (emotion) feeling.

SE: I feel (emotion) when I think of eating intuitively

UE: I don't think I can trust myself.

UN: This (emotion) feeling that makes me so uncomfortable.

CHIN: This feeling of (emotion) at the thought of eating intuitively — what if I get fat?

CB: What if it doesn't work.

UA: I don't think I can trust my intuition, what if I am wrong.

TH: This overwhelming feeling of (emotion).

See if you can link any patterns or memories around how food has impacted on your life. The times in the past when you felt out of control, or you felt like you had failed at losing weight in the past (If not just continue tapping on the feeling)

Repeat one more time and then take a deep breath and measure the level of intensity in your body.

Once you are happy that the level of emotion has dropped to a 2-0 — you can begin the Reframe Round.

Reframe Reclaim Round

Set-Up Statement: Even though I had this uncomfortable feeling, which is now a level (new level of intensity), I choose now to be comfortable and confident, allowing myself to eat anything I want, and trust in my intuition. I deeply and completely accept this new belief.

Set-Up Statement: Even though the words *I now allow myself to eat anything I want, I now honor my body* feel a little scary still, I deeply and completely accept this new belief in me.

Set-Up Statement: Even though I have released the intensity of fear around trusting my intuition, I now choose to be open to other limiting beliefs, and I choose to reclaim the beliefs that empower me, and attract opportunities into my life in many ways. And I deeply and completely accept this new belief.

EB: I choose to allow myself to eat anything I want; What does my body really want?

SE: I choose to allow myself to eat anything I want; I honor my body at all times.

UE: I choose to allow myself to eat anything I want; What does my body really want?

UN: I choose to allow myself to eat anything I want; I honor my body at all times.

CHIN: I choose to allow myself to eat anything I want; What does my body really want?

CB: I am now grateful for the way my body chooses foods that enhance my energy, vitality and confidence.

UA: I am so grateful for the way in which the food I choose creates vibrant health and energy.

TH: I am so grateful for the way my body responds to this new way to eating, and I choose to trust my intuition always.

The Power Pose

Now stand with your hands on your hips, feet slightly apart (you can do this physically, or just imagine yourself doing it.) Imagine that you are standing in the most powerful position you can. Your shoulders are back, your spine is straight.

Use the powerful affirmation *I choose to allow myself to eat anything I want; What does my body really want"*

Imagine that you are drawing up all the confidence, power and forgiveness you need through your feet and up into your heart. Then imagine that all that new energy is being distributed to every cell in your body. Hold this pose (or the image of this pose for about 1 to 2 minutes, until you can feel this new energy powering in your body).

It helps to write down any feelings, memories or emotions that arose during the tapping, and in the next chapter I will explain why the process of journaling is so powerful.

EFT is not a one of practice, but something to do every day whenever you feel a negative emotion arises. I recommend that in the beginning you use EFT every day, while it becomes a habit. And pretty soon you will be tapping on every feeling thing - no matter who is watching or where you are! You will learn to feel the power of it, and how the habit of practicing it daily can change your life.

Acknowledgements

My sincere and grateful thanks to the following people who helped make this book a reality:

To Alissa Guignard and Megan Sutton. Thank you for your suggestions, your input and editing skills.

To my husband Gerry for his artistic talents and patience in creation of the book cover and formatting.

Thanks to Glen Calizon, Jenn Antonio and the team at Lykos Studios for the rebranding of the website and ongoing support in helping bring the brand Mid-Life Reimagined to life.

To Rob Gilbert, for the wonderful photos used for the cover and website.

And finally, to the women I have supported, presented to and coached over the last 15 years. Your stories have helped shape the 10 Principles into the powerful tool it is today, together we are re-imagining midlife, with strength, clarity and unapologetic confidence.

About Sally Thibault

Sally is an Australian award-winning keynote speaker, best-selling author, podcast host and menopause in the workplace workshop facilitator, now living in Canada. She is dedicated to empowering women to navigate midlife challenges with confidence and balance. With over 40 years of experience in the fitness industry as a gym owner, instructor trainer, TV show host and media commentator Sally brings a wealth of knowledge and a proven track record of inspiring transformation.

Specialising in the unique journey of helping women leaders navigate mid-life and the menopause transition, she integrates holistic approaches that address emotional, physical, and mental well-being. With a strong background in counselling, coaching and as a professional speaker & workshop facilitator, Sally employs powerful wisdom, experience and her signature 10 Principles of Wellness, to help women step into their true power.

Known for her expertise in simple wellness strategies and purpose redefinition during midlife transitions, Sally uses her own experiences to guide others through this transformative period. Through her books, dynamic speaking engagements, menopause in the workplace workshops and group coaching programs, she inspires women to embrace midlife as an opportunity for profound personal growth and empowerment to be strong, clear and unapologetic leaders.

Discover how you can reclaim your energy, redefine your purpose, and thrive in every area of your life with guidance from a true industry veteran and transformational leader.

Sally has been married to her husband since 1982. She is a proud mother of three adult children and also a proud grandmother of baby Ava.

Sally's Website https://www.mid-lifereimagined.com

For details about booking Sally to speak at your event, or facilitate a *Menopause in the Workplace* workshop, please email her team at **info@mid-lifereimagined.com**

Other Books by Sally Thibault

David's Gift, Aspergers Life & Love
https://amzn.to/4iQJZYT

Tapping To Reclaim You - *Reignite Your Passion Power & Purpose in 30 Days* https://bit.ly/41LAZ0l

Social Media

Facebook https://www.facebook.com/sallythibaut1

Instagram https://www.instagram.com/sallythibault

LinkedIn: https://www.linkedin.com/in/sallythibault

You Tube https://www.youtube.com/@SallyThibault

For details of the 9Minute Workout Series
https://www.9minworkout.com/rego

References

New Research on How Women in Leadership Navigated Menopause - Mallory Decker and Alicia A. Grandey: https://hbr.org/2025/11/new-research-on-how-women-in-leadership-navigated-menopause

Fast Like A Girl, Dr Mindy Pelz.
https://www.mindypelz.com

Atomic Habits - An easy and proven way to build good habits and break bad ones

Author James Clear https://jamesclear.com/

You Can Heal Your Life Author Louise Hay
https://www.louisehay.com/

Dr Roger Callahan, Thought Field Therapy
http://www.rogercallahan.com

Gary Craig, www.emofree.com

Dr Dawson Church
https://www.eftuniverse.com/research-studies

Dr Joe Dispenza You Are the Placebo: Making Your Mind Matter   https://www.drjoedispenza.com/

The Calorie King Website https://www.calorieking.com

EFT Universe Research

https://eftuniverse.com/index.php?option=com_content&view=article&id=18

Headspace.com https://www.headspace.com/science

Scientific American - What does mindfulness do to your brain?

https://blogs.scientificamerican.com/guest-blog/what-does-mindfulness-meditation-do-to-your-brain/

How to have more positive thoughts The Tlex Institute

https://tlexinstitute.com/how-to-effortlessly-have-more-positive-thoughts/

The Happiness Advantage Author Shawn Achor
http://www.shawnachor.com

Men are from Mars Women are From Venus -

Author Dr John Grey https://www.marsvenus.com/

The Imposter Syndrome in High Achieving Women Dr. Pauline R. Clance & Dr Suzanne A Imes
https://psycnet.apa.org/record/1979-26502-001

The Secret Thoughts of Successful Women

Dr Valerie Young   https://impostorsyndrome.com/

The Gifts of Imperfection – Author Dr.Brene Brown.
www.brenebrown.com

The Me Too Movement
https://en.wikipedia.org/wiki/Me_Too_movement

 Super Soul Podcast, Dr. Edith Eva Eger, The Choice, 24/6/29 www.supersoulconversations.com

Rising Strong – Author Dr Brene Brown
www.brenebrown.com

What is Confirmation Bias, People are prone to believe what they want to believe

Dr Sharam Hashmat

https://www.psychologytoday.com/au/blog/science-choice/201504/what-is-confirmation-bias

Telomeres, lifestyle, cancer, and aging; Masood A. Shammas

https://www.ncbi.nlm.nih.gov/pmc/articles/PMC3370421/

The effect of high intensity interval training on telomere length and telomerase activity in non-athlete young men

https://www.researchgate.net/publication/325134827_The_effect_of_high_intensity_interval_training_on_telomere_length_and_telomerase_activity_in_non-athlete_young_men

Experts: Exercise Will Actually Make Your Cells Younger and Life Longer; The Hearty Soul May 2018

https://theheartysoul.com/telomeres-and-aging-exercise-lengthens-telomeres/

Earth-shattering' study reveals the best exercise for anti-ageing, Sydney Morning Herald 28 March 2017

https://www.smh.com.au/lifestyle/health-and-wellness/earthshattering-study-reveals-the-best-exercise-for-antiageing-20170328-gv7yx2.html

Benefits of High Intensity Interval Training (HIIT); Dr Axe Food Is Medicine 12 May 2016 https://draxe.com/fitness/workouts/benefits-high-intensity-interval-training/

7 Ways Strength Training Boosts Your Health and Fitness; Every Day Heath 5 May 2019

https://www.everydayhealth.com/fitness/add-strength-training-to-your-workout.aspx

Add Strength Training to Your Fitness Plan; Harvard Health Publishing May 2015

https://www.health.harvard.edu/staying-healthy/add-strength-training-to-your-fitness-plan

Intermittent Fasting the Science of Going Without

https://www.ncbi.nlm.nih.gov/pmc/articles/PMC3680567

Intermittent fasting boosts health by strengthening daily rhythms. Medical News Today

https://www.medicalnewstoday.com/articles

Are you a fast eater? May 2018

https://health.clevelandclinic.org/are-you-a-fast-eater-slow-down-to-eat-and-weigh-less/

Slow down You Eat Too Fast   Kathleen M. Zelman, MPH, RD, LD

https://www.webmd.com/diet/obesity/features/slow-down-you-eat-too-fast

Your Body Needs Time off alcohol Simone Strasser Sydney Morning Herald January 29, 2015

https://www.smh.com.au/lifestyle/health-and-wellness/why-your-body-loves-time-off-from-alcohol-especially-if-youre-female

www.eft.com.au

www.thetappingsolution.com

www.drjoedispenza.com

https://patcarrington.com/

Amy Cuddy – Your Body Language May Shape Who You are

https://www.ted.com/talks/amy_cuddy_your_body_language_shapes_who_you_are

www.ingramcontent.com/pod-product-compliance
Lightning Source LLC
LaVergne TN
LVHW051255080426
835509LV00020B/2982